Advance praise for *The New York Mets All-Time All-Stars*

"Mets fans will love digging into *The New York Mets All-Time All-Stars*. From the obvious picks to a few surprises, the book highlights the franchise's best in a breezy, easy-to-read style."

—Tom Verducci, *New York Times* best-selling
author, Fox and MLB network analyst

"Tom Seaver. Check. Mike Piazza. Check. Keith Hernandez. Check. The Mets marquee All-Stars are here, but Brian Wright digs deep to make his case for all the Mets—and any owner, front office executive, or manager—who made the cut. What better way to enjoy the greatest Mets milestones and moments than through the 'All-Time All-Stars' who actually made them happen? Their stories are expertly brought to life in this fun journey through Mets history."

—Bob Heussler, WFAN

"Brian definitely brought back memories of my days with the Mets and some of the characters I was privileged to play alongside. It was fun to read."

—Jon Matlack, 1972 National League Rookie
of the Year and three-time All-Star

"There's no debating Tom Seaver is the greatest Mets star of all time, but where do the other franchise luminaries rank? Brian Wright does a terrific and thorough job of making strong and compelling cases for the legends who have captured the hearts of Mets fans since 1962."

—Gary Apple, SNY Mets pre- and postgame TV host

"I believe this book captures the details that will keep any Mets fan thoroughly entertained. I read it, and I definitely was. It is an honor to be included in this fine work."

—Howard Johnson, 1986 World Series champion and two-time All-Star

"Like a pennant-winning manager of yore, Brian Wright knows which Mets he's going to take on his All-Star team and doesn't mind telling you why. His bold selection process would make Gil Hodges and Davey Johnson proud."

—Greg Prince, author of *Faith and Fear in Flushing*

"Brian is a knowledgeable historian who does his homework to make sure he gets it right. And as a Mets fan he knows New Yorkers will be right there to tell him *their* opinions."

—Matt Silverman, author of *100 Things Mets Fans Should Know & Do Before They Die* and *Swinging '73*

THE NEW YORK METS ALL-TIME ALL-STARS

THE BEST PLAYERS AT EACH POSITION FOR THE AMAZIN'S

BRIAN WRIGHT

LYONS
PRESS

Guilford, Connecticut

*To the friends and family who have tolerated
my obsession all these years*

An imprint of The Rowman & Littlefield Publishing Group, Inc.
4501 Forbes Blvd., Ste. 200
Lanham, MD 20706
www.rowman.com

Distributed by NATIONAL BOOK NETWORK

British Library Cataloguing in Publication Information available

Library of Congress Cataloging-in-Publication Data

Names: Wright, Brian (Baseball writer), author.
Title: The New York Mets all-time all-stars : the best players at each
  position for the Amazin's / Brian Wright.
Description: Guilford, Connecticut : Lyons Press, 2020. | Includes
  bibliographical references. | Summary: "Combining statistical analysis,
  common sense, and a host of intangibles, Brian Wright constructs an
  all-time All-Star Mets line-up for the ages"— Provided by publisher.
Identifiers: LCCN 2019042932 (print) | LCCN 2019042933 (ebook) | ISBN
  9781493046621 (paperback) | ISBN 9781493046638 (epub)
Subjects: LCSH: New York Mets (Baseball team)—History. | Baseball
  players--New York (State)—New York—Biography.
Classification: LCC GV875.N45 W683 2020 (print) | LCC GV875.N45 (ebook) |
  DDC 796.357/64097471—dc23
LC record available at https://lccn.loc.gov/2019042932
LC ebook record available at https://lccn.loc.gov/2019042933

CONTENTS

INTRODUCTION

"Can't anybody here play this game?"

That was the unsuccessful plea allegedly uttered by manager Casey Stengel, remarking on his 1962 New York Mets' astounding ineptitude. New York's current National League franchise came to life that year. And like all newborns, they needed to crawl before they could walk.

This phase appeared interminable, fraught with stumbles and falls unmatched in baseball history.

The length and breadth of the Mets' struggles, and the subjects of such folly, became legendary in the tall tales of their meager beginnings. There was "Marvelous" Marv Throneberry, fielding grounders with his eyes closed; Harry Chiti, the catcher New York obtained from the Indians in exchange for a player to be named later only to be so unpolished that the Mets sent him back to Cleveland 30 days later; Roger Craig, who found himself pitching just well enough to lose 18 straight decisions; "Choo-Choo" Coleman, who sufficed for a catcher amid ground-level expectations; and the not-so-aptly-named "Hot" Rod Kanehl.

This kaleidoscope of calamity proved more endearing than embarrassing. Filling the void left by the departure of the Giants and Dodgers in 1957, fans who longed for a replacement embraced the Mets as their beloved new major-league outfit, even though it was difficult to believe this qualified as major-league material. They grew up suddenly by the end of the decade, culminating in the most improbable World Series triumph and helping to supply a healthy portion of talent for this Mets All-Time All-Star team.

From "Tom Terrific" to "Doctor K" to "The Captain" and everyone in between, the history of the Mets is told through the stories of the 35 brightest stars in the constellation of baseball in Queens.

The full team consists of 30 players, a manager, two coaches, a general manager, and an owner. The players are broken down this way: 10 pitchers (without any focus on specializations), three catchers, 10 infielders, and seven outfielders. Seventeen players who didn't quite make the cut are listed as honorable mentions, while the two coaches on the team are the runners-up for manager.

Now that we know the 'who,' what about the 'how?'

Baseball is a sport which lends itself well to generational comparisons and debates. Both are in abundant supply when selecting the ideal Mets roster. The criteria for inclusion are based on a combination of intangibles, accolades, Mets career numbers, and prestige/impact on the organization. Traditional statistics—like home runs, runs batted in (RBIs), batting average, and earned run average (ERA)—were naturally utilized in evaluating each player. The weight of certain measures—pitching wins, especially—vary depending on time period. Also used were more advanced metrics that delve deeper into a players' value and take into account specific variables, allowing for better comparisons across eras. Such sabermetric-friendly statistics include:

- **Wins Above Replacement (WAR):** measures a player's value by determining how many more wins that player is worth versus a replacement-level player at the same position. As a barometer for what constitutes excellence in this category, Jacob deGrom led the Mets in 2019 at 7.9 according to Baseball-Reference.

- **Walks and Hits per Innings Pitched (WHIP):** today considered one of the most commonly used statistics to evaluate pitcher performance, this shows how well they keep opponents off the bases.

- **Adjusted ERA (ERA+):** alters a pitcher's ERA according to the ballpark and the ERA of the pitcher's league. An ERA+ of 100 is designated as the league baseline.

- **Fielding Independent Pitching (FIP):** uses the three events a pitcher can most control (home runs, walks, strikeouts) and converts them into a number. Like ERA+, a FIP of 100 is equal to the league average.

- **Fielding Runs:** the number of runs saved based on the number of plays made.

- **Range Factor:** calculated by dividing the sum of a fielder's putouts and assists by the total number of defensive games played.

- **Ultimate Zone Rating (UZR):** another fielding measurement, this attempts to quantify the number of runs a player saved or allowed through their fielding prowess.

- **On-Base Plus Slugging (OPS):** a combination of how well a player can reach base with how well that player can hit for power and average. An enhanced version of this stat is OPS+, which takes into account external factors such as ballparks.

- **Runs Created:** estimates a player's offensive contribution in terms of total runs. It combines a player's ability to get on base with his ability to hit for extra bases, then divides them by the player's total opportunities. This number can be adjusted based on factors like park and time period to create a stat called Weighted Runs Created Plus (wRC+).

The hope is that these choices, and how they are chosen, will foster debates—not end them. Some of the selections for the Mets All-Time All-Star team won't be surprising. Some might not be to everyone's liking. But collectively, each have had a part in the best moments of a unique six-decade history. Being a Mets fan tests faith, incites passion, and builds character. The people you'll read about have made this enthralling and sometimes bewildering exercise more worthwhile.

That said, it's now time to meet the Mets.

1

PITCHERS

Starting Pitcher—Tom Seaver

The argument for the greatest Met ever isn't an argument at all. Seaver rewrote the Mets history book with his golden right arm, leaving an indelible mark on this team that will be almost impossible to erase. It would be less exhausting to recount the team pitching records he *doesn't* hold. No. 41 is first in wins, strikeouts, complete games, shutouts, ERA, and All-Star appearances.

But numbers and rankings don't convey his full impact. Simply put, Seaver transformed the identity of an organization—doing so with an intense competitive drive and a scientific study of pitching. He examined the mechanics of his throwing motion, the art of keeping opposing hitters off-balance, and the understanding of each batter's weakness. Never was Seaver going to be outsmarted or outworked. Such diligence rubbed off on those around him.

"When we started getting the feeling of competitiveness, it was all about learning how to win close games," outfielder Art Shamsky said. "We were going to be close every time he pitched, and Tom gave us confidence we could win those games."

The Mets spent their initial five years with nary a sense of direction. And if not for an unusual sequence of events that ended with a favorable luck of the draw, he wouldn't have been the one to provide it.

After multiple attempts for other teams to draft him fell through, Major League Baseball set up a special lottery for the former University of Southern California product under one condition: pony up at least $50,000. Three clubs had the payroll and the foresight to meet that threshold: the Phillies, Indians, and Mets. Three pieces of paper—representing the teams vying for Seaver's services—went into a hat. You can figure out the rest.

This serendipitous match between New York and the right-hander from Fresno provided the backdrop to an unparalleled career. For more than a decade, Seaver and the Mets were synonymous.

The style and substance that defined Seaver's baseball persona was readily apparent soon after his major-league career began at the start of the 1967 season. In a city where the media eats youngsters for lunch, Seaver demonstrated maturity that belied his age. "Even though he was a rookie, he was so far ahead of the hitters (mentally), it was unbelievable," catcher Jerry Grote said.

During that time, first-year players were seen and seldom heard. Seaver quickly harnessed the attention of the public with 16 wins on a team that totaled only 61, posted an ERA of 2.76, and struck out 170. He was the lone Mets representative in that year's All-Star Game and spoke to the press with the eloquence and assurance for which he was so noted.

Seaver's Rookie of the Year performance laid the foundation for his upcoming brilliance. What followed would be a beautiful 11-season portrait. Seaver was the artist, the pitching mound his studio. His masterpieces are stored in the Mets historical vault like paintings in the Louvre. Two of his works stand above the rest.

He asserted his usual dominance against the San Diego Padres on April 22, 1970, then took it to a new level. Beginning with the final out of the sixth inning, Seaver proceeded to close with a historical flourish. Nobody reached base. Nobody put the ball in play. When he fanned Al Ferrara to end the top of the ninth, Seaver had struck out 19—tying a major-league record at the time. But his 10 consecutive strikeouts—to end the game, no less—is a record that has never been matched.

It was on this afternoon when Seaver received his 1969 Cy Young Award. And July 9 of the previous year was the best example of why he earned that honor.

In front of a jam-packed Shea Stadium, Seaver went through the first 25 Chicago Cubs batters unscathed. The electricity from the raucous sold-out crowd amplified as the string of outs accumulated. Seaver calls it his best game, but also his "Imperfect Game." Imperfect because of Jimmy Qualls—a man who had 11 big-league hits to date and who would end up with only 31 for his career. Qualls etched his name in Mets lore with a clean single to left-center—denying Seaver's dream of perfection. Dreams of a World Series title, however, were soon to be realized.

It had seemed unimaginable prior to '69. When the Mets surprisingly reached .500 in May, Tom made it clear he wasn't in the mood for celebration. There was no reason to rejoice in such small victories, like they might have done before. Seaver was determined to help put the Mets' days of despair behind them.

The Mets enjoyed numerous contributions throughout the course of their improbable journey—Tommie Agee patrolling

Tom Seaver is the standard by which all Mets are measured.
JERRY COLI/DREAMSTIME

center field with his magical glove, Donn Clendenon revitalizing the lineup after being traded to Queens in June, a rotation fortified by Jerry Koosman and Gary Gentry, and a bullpen headed by Tug McGraw and Ron Taylor. But Seaver was the star around which the rest of the team orbited.

While he carried the fortunes of the Mets in his capable pitching arm, it was Gil Hodges who called the shots. Seaver—who, like Hodges, had served in the Marines—echoed the word of his manager's straightforward gospel.

"Gil was a very dominant man," Seaver said. "It was quite an experience playing for a man who was as strong in his feelings as Gil was, who believed in his feelings on baseball, his thoughts on baseball, and how baseball should be played."

In 1968, the first year with Hodges at the Mets helm, Seaver showed steady improvement from his rookie campaign. He lowered his ERA to 2.20 and his WHIP to 0.978 while achieving the first of several 200-plus strikeout seasons.

Both Hodges and pitching coach Rube Walker, the two biggest influences on the development of Seaver's career, leaned heavily on education by way of repetition and correction.

"The biggest thing that they did was they gave you the ball," Seaver said. "You learned by pitching. And then you try to dissect your mistakes ... and as you go through the course of a career, then you intellectually begin to understand what you're doing mentally and physically."

By the summer of 1969, the duo of Seaver and second-year left-hander Jerry Koosman had already acquired a wealth of knowledge.

The next three months proved Seaver had attained mastery. From August 9 through the end of the regular season, he made 11 starts and went 10-0—eight of which were complete games. His ERA during this crucial stretch was a microscopic 1.34. On September 9, Seaver went the distance against Chicago as the Mets closed in on the Cubs in the NL East race. New York passed them for good the next night. The Mets stayed so hot, they even withstood two lackluster Seaver starts in the post-season—first in the opening game of the inaugural National League Championship Series in Atlanta (which turned into a win) and then in the World Series opener at Baltimore. Seaver redeemed himself in Game 4 by limiting the vaunted Orioles offense to one run over 10 innings with the help of Ron Swoboda's sprawling ninth-inning catch. One day later, the impossible dream came true in the form of a world championship.

Not long after the ticker tape fell in lower Manhattan, individual adulations poured in. A 25-7 record and a 2.21 ERA were numbers worthy of a well-earned Cy Young Award and nearly the league MVP—falling short of the Giants' Willie McCovey. *Sports Illustrated* later recognized him as its Sportsman of the Year. But beyond those distinctions came even more distinguished notoriety.

New York had unofficially inducted its newest sporting legend—fully embracing Seaver's intelligence, integrity, and intensity in a city that thrives on such qualities. His legend only grew in the post-championship years—the three most overpowering seasons of his career.

From 1970–72, Seaver fanned an average of 274 batters, led the NL in strikeouts twice, and claimed a pair of ERA titles. Still, somehow, he never added to his Cy Young collection. The most galling omission came in 1971. Seaver constructed a career-low 1.76 ERA, a career-low 0.946 WHIP, a career-high 289 strikeouts, and a career-best 9.1 K's per nine innings. Each of those figures were atop the league leaderboard at year's end. But the weight of wins tipped the scales in favor of Chicago's Ferguson Jenkins, who tallied 24 victories to Seaver's 20.

There would be no snub in 1973, a season in which he kept the Mets afloat amid a deluge of injuries. Only twice did Seaver allow more than four runs in a start. And by mid-September, a replenished roster sparked a resurgence. Even as Seaver's shoulder barked with soreness, the call of the pennant race didn't go unanswered. Seaver locked up the division and the Cy Young in Chicago with the help of Tug McGraw to earn his 19th win and secure an MLB-best 2.08 ERA.

He then attempted to win the NLCS opener in Cincinnati on his own—responsible for the lone Mets run and keeping

New York tied through eight innings. But he was done in by Johnny Bench's walk-off homer. Seaver got another crack at the Reds in Game 5 with the World Series at stake. He wasn't nearly as sharp (striking out four and walking five), but he didn't need to be. Given a 7–2 lead, Seaver again passed the baton over to McGraw, who took the Mets across the finish line.

By pitching the NLCS finale, Seaver was available for only two World Series appearances. Both starts came with their own bit of frustration. He exited Game 3 tied after eight innings—a contest Oakland eventually won in 11. As the Mets took the next two at Shea, Seaver was set for a potential close-out start in the Bay Area. With the luxury of a series lead, manager Yogi Berra weighed his options. He could go with his best, Seaver, or his freshest, George Stone—12-3 during the regular season—and preserve Tom an extra day if Game 7 presented itself. Berra played his ace, sore shoulder be damned. Seaver pitched well over seven innings, allowing two runs. His opponent, Catfish Hunter, pitched slightly better—one run over 7.1 innings. The result of that day and the next (both in Oakland's favor) made Berra's decision dubious, forever fostering debate as to whether the alternative would've yielded a different outcome.

Through seven seasons, Seaver had assembled a career worthy of mention among the all-time greats: an average of 19 wins and 236 strikeouts, a splendid 2.38 ERA, along with 121 complete games and 24 shutouts. So when he finished 1974 at 11-11 with a 3.20 ERA—a final stat line most pitchers would envy—it felt second-rate. Such were the standards for a pitcher of his caliber.

It indeed was an outlier from the expected brilliance. But, in fairness, his body didn't cooperate. To say his year was a pain in the butt was not a figure of speech. A strained sciatic nerve on the left part of his backside forced multiple stints on the mend and severely curtailed hopes for a productive year.

Of sound body and mind, Seaver rebounded in 1975 back on-brand. During a season in which he went 22-9 and won his third Cy Young, he attained two significant strikeout milestones. First, reaching 2,000 for his career and, later, becoming the first pitcher to fan at least 200 in eight consecutive seasons.

Leave it to M. Donald Grant to ruin a great thing. June 15, 1977, is a date that lives in Mets infamy. A date when the stubbornness of the team's two most prominent figures reached its tipping point. A date that set the organization back for years to come.

Owner Joan Payson's passing in 1975 coupled with Gil Hodges's death in 1972 erased Tom's sources of comfort. The bulk of the decision-making was in the less-than-capable hands of Grant. The team chairman expressed little to no interest during the advent of free agency and scoffed at Seaver's demands for more money. To Grant, players of Seaver's ilk were more arrogant than dignified. He was unwilling to understand the changing lifestyles of the modern athlete and publicly aired his grievances regarding his star pitcher's wishes to be paid to the level of his immense value.

The sides did agree to a modest contract extension, but Tom was still disturbed by the paucity of Met free-agent signings. When a 2.59 ERA and a league-best 235 strikeouts could only equal a 14-11 record in 1976, it did little to curb his frustrations.

Grant wasn't alone in challenging the face of the Mets. He had a powerful voice taking up his argument. Dick Young, the legendary and cantankerous columnist for the *New York Daily*

News, shared Grant's disdain for free agency and regularly wrote with scorn for Seaver.

Tom went into 1977 disgruntled and continued to pitch with little support, but had secretly worked out a three-year extension with Lorinda de Roulet two days before the June 15 trade deadline.

But on that fateful day, Young dropped an atomic bomb. His latest column alleged that Tom's wife, Nancy, was jealous of Nolan Ryan's wife, Ruth, because his former teammate was earning a higher salary with the California Angels. Call it the match to the powder keg.

Seaver asked out of New York. The Mets bent to his demand, sending him to the Cincinnati Reds and letting the proverbial wrecking ball loose on what is now known as the "Midnight Massacre." The cumulative WAR for the four players the Mets received over their careers in New York (12.3 combined) was only slightly above Seaver's best season (11.0 in 1973). And it certainly couldn't measure up to his stature. Naturally, the Mets took a nosedive into irrelevance.

Time passed, however, and Grant departed as the ultimate Mets villain. Queens now became a safe harbor for Seaver under the right conditions. They were in the winter of 1982, when the Reds dealt him back to New York.

At age 38, by baseball standards, he was an old Tom Seaver. But when he took the mound on Opening Day 1983 against Philadelphia—a glorious sun-drenched afternoon dripping with nostalgia—a packed Shea Stadium got to witness something resembling the Tom Seaver of old. He shut out the Phillies for six innings in a vintage performance. But before you could even conceive a full-circle finish to his career, the Mets somehow found another way to let Seaver go.

On the verge of his 300th win, Seaver was left unprotected in a free-agent compensation pool in January 1984. Much to the Mets' surprise, the White Sox nabbed him.

Soon after he called it quits on a two-decade career, the well-deserved post-retirement honors poured in. Some were appropriately swift—like the retirement of his No. 41 and the resounding, near-unanimous first-ballot induction into the Hall of Fame. Some came far too late—namely the statue outside Citi Field.

While his pitching days were behind him, he found a lifestyle where he could continue to hone his precision: running a vineyard. "Same thing as pitching—attention to detail," he said in 2014. "You can't force it. It's a lot of fun."

But even ordinary physical and mental abilities have recently left him. It was revealed in 2019 that Seaver has dementia—stemming from the contraction of Lyme disease decades earlier—and thus was retiring from public life. It was a cruel diagnosis to someone renowned for his combination of strength and acumen. The news elicited memories from those of a certain generation who could vividly recall the countless outstanding performances, the signature drop-and-drive motion, and the incomparable influence he had on the fortunes of the Mets. It was a clear reminder that he is without equal in team history. Tom Seaver will be known as "The Franchise" as long as there is one.

Starting Pitcher—Dwight Gooden

The year was 1984. Fans who once dreaded going to Shea Stadium were now coming in droves. Those who occupied a section in the left-field corner hung "K" signs with each strikeout he racked up. And there were a lot of them. He kept everyone in his purview enthralled—fans, teammates, and those unlucky enough to face him. When the young man they called "Dr. K" was at his best, it was hard to envision anyone better.

There is a direct correlation between the Tom Seaver trade in June 1977 and the moment when Shea, for all intents and purposes, went dark. While Keith Hernandez and Darryl Strawberry brought attitude and power, respectively, when they arrived in 1983, it was Gooden—at a mere 19 years old—who brought the electricity back.

Shea was a baseball mortuary for seven long years, as fan support diminished and victories became even scarcer. Now it was host to must-see off-Broadway theater. The lead performer was a captivating pitching wunderkind. Not just the most exciting teenager in the big leagues but arguably the top pitcher in baseball.

The every-fifth-day prescription Doc doled out to his elders was comprised of a whistling high-90s fastball countered with a drop-off-the-table curveball so effective that it carried the reverent moniker of "Lord Charles." Helpless opponents were given the grim choice of being overpowered by heat or fooled by his breaking pitch.

The end results for 1984 were remarkable. Gooden's 276 strikeouts (11.4 every nine innings) is a rookie record that still stands. Of the 879 batters he faced, 31.4 percent ended with a K.

If Gooden at age 19 was a revelation, Gooden at age 20 was nothing short of extraordinary: 24-4 with a 1.53 ERA and 268 punchouts—the best season this pitching-rich franchise has ever seen.

He would go on to win 157 times and record 1,875 K's over his 11 seasons, placing Gooden on the short list of best Mets arms. If you were devising a Mount Rushmore of Mets, Gooden could easily be among that quartet. You could even make a case that his No. 16 should be retired. But the story of Gooden will forever be told as a cautionary tale—one in which outside influences and internal demons stunted his astonishing talents and prevented him from achieving even greater accomplishments. His career is as much about what could have been as what was.

Gooden's meteoric rise to stardom began in the spring of 1983, when the first-round pick of the year before started the season in Double-A. By September, he was pitching the Davey Johnson–led Triple-A club through the minor-league playoffs.

General manager Frank Cashen insisted Gooden remain in the minors to start 1984. Johnson, who was promoted to Mets manager, insisted Doc was major-league ready. Davey won that argument. Soon enough, there was no questioning the decision.

Within three months, Gooden was a local and national sensation, leading the league in strikeouts while barely old enough to vote. His starts at Shea became akin to rock concerts. Fans wanted to watch the teenage pitching sensation as much as they wanted to watch the Mets. A national audience got to see what everyone in New York was buzzing about. Gooden became the youngest All-Star selection ever and proved he wasn't fazed by the added spotlight. Doc struck out three American Leaguers in succession and went two scoreless innings.

The rookie phenomenon reached his peak in early September against the Cubs, who were leading the NL East by seven games over New York. Gooden, who would end '84 with a 2.60 ERA and a 17-9 record, unleashed a heavy dosage of his bewildering arsenal. He struck out 11, allowing just one hit and four walks, in a complete game shutout. That night was a preview to an awe-inspiring Cy Young exhibition in 1985.

Dwight Gooden won the 1985 Cy Young Award with the finest pitching season in Mets history.

Gooden dispensed with any sophomore slump in the same manner he continued to cast aside National League hitters who hadn't caught up with him.

"Every game I was feeling locked in," he said. "It just felt like every game I was going to win."

By August 25, he had as many victories as life years, becoming the youngest to reach that 20-win plateau. His 24th and final victory came against the Cardinals in a must-win contest, with hopes fading for a division title. The Mets finished second, but Gooden was first in just about every notable pitching category.

His lofty win total, ultra-low ERA, and high strikeout count were enough to give him the pitching equivalent of the Triple Crown. A Rookie of the Year award followed by a Cy Young plaque earned Gooden effusive praise from former All-Stars and Hall of Famers alike.

When asked to describe Doc, ex–Oakland A's lefty Vida Blue succinctly said: "bona fide." Dodgers immortal Sandy Koufax heaped more praise: "I'd trade my past for his future." His potential seemed limitless.

For the remainder of the decade, while he stayed the ace of the staff and made four All-Star teams (twice as the starter), Gooden's glow began to fade a bit. Some seasons were more humbling than others. As special as 1986 was for the Mets, it was the year in which the initial cracks in Gooden's seemingly impenetrable facade began to surface.

Pitching coach Mel Stottlemyre instructed Gooden to incorporate a changeup to complement his blistering fastball and 12-to-6 curve. Doc didn't strike out batters as frequently, but he still became the first pitcher to fan at least 200 in each of his first three seasons. He was 17-6 with a 2.84 ERA, a pedestrian stat line in comparison to the previous year—but just about anything would have been. Surrounded by a rotation and lineup with few holes, the Mets sailed to the division title—one which Doc clinched on September 17 with a complete game effort against Chicago.

As Gooden embarked on the first of six postseason starts as a Met, he'd soon find October had its own challenges. In the NLCS opener, he wound up on the short end of 14-strikeout master Mike Scott. In Game 5, with the series tied at two, Doc matched zeroes with veteran Nolan Ryan. Gooden went 10 innings but left tied at one.

The World Series was a whole different story. A much-anticipated duel against fellow fireballer Roger Clemens in Game 2 flamed out quickly. Gooden allowed five runs in five innings. Things weren't much better four days later at Fenway—falling into a 3–0 hole before being pulled in the fifth.

Although the Mets overcame those setbacks, Gooden would not. He missed the celebratory parade the day following the Game 7 win. Initially, everyone thought he overslept. The real reason was drugs. Rumors had surfaced earlier in the year that an African American superstar on the Mets had been using cocaine. No one believed it was Gooden, who appeared to the public to be a youngster with stable parental support and a level head. But by April 1, 1987, those rumors were verified. At spring training, he tested positive for cocaine. A 60-day suspension by MLB—including entrance into a rehabilitation clinic—kept him out of action for the first two months.

Fans were willing to forgive his personal faults. Most of the capacity crowd in his return to the Shea Stadium mound on June 5 offered Gooden a standing ovation. They did so again when he departed after giving up four hits and one earned run and striking out five over 6.2 innings. Gooden went on to win seven of his first nine starts.

Despite success, his strikeout rate was on the decline and dipped further still in 1988. He only fanned 6.3 per nine innings but won at least 18 games for the first time since '85. With a much healthier staff than the previous year, the Mets returned to the playoffs. As staff ace, Gooden was again called to take on the best arms. This time, it was the Dodgers' Orel Hershiser, fresh off a record-setting 59 consecutive scoreless innings to finish the regular season. In Game 1, Gooden left trailing 2–0 after seven innings but having struck out 10. The Mets rallied to win that night and held a 2-1 series lead with Gooden on the hill for Game 4.

After relinquishing a pair of early runs, he kept the visiting Dodgers on lock down. The Mets went up 4–2 as their right-hander assumed total command—not having allowed a hit since the first inning. Three outs from putting Los Angeles on the doorstep of elimination, Gooden let leadoff hitter John Shelby walk after starting him 0-2. Next was Mike Scioscia— an unimposing contact-hitting catcher with 35 homers in eight and a half years. Gooden made sure to get the first pitch over the plate. Scioscia connected and stunned everyone when his drive cleared the right-field wall. Just like that, Gooden's dominance evaporated. Los Angeles's comeback, finished in the 12th inning, confirmed what may have been the most gut-wrenching defeat in franchise history. It certainly was the toughest on-field setback of Gooden's career. New York could never truly recover as the Dodgers took the series in seven.

The toll of so many innings at a young age began to rear its head. Gooden labored to a 9-4 record in 1989 and an ERA a shade under 3.00 before shoulder discomfort put him on the disabled list—first for a couple weeks, then for a couple months. When he returned, Doc was relegated to relief appearances.

Gooden lost five of his first eight decisions in 1990, and despite rattling off 15 victories in 17 tries, his 3.90 ERA was the highest of his career. He'd end up with his best win total since 1985 and joined David Cone as one of two Mets starters to eclipse 200 strikeouts. As Darryl Strawberry departed via free agency, the organization knew Doc was one they couldn't afford to let get away. In the offseason, it paid him like an ace, but he never would be one again.

The Gooden of '91 wasn't the Gooden of 1984, '85, or even '86. Still, at 13-7 and with a 3.60 ERA, he remained a reliable starter and a reminder of a time long since gone. That was until August 22, when a shoulder stiffness became the cause for rotator cuff surgery.

He recovered decently, posting a 3.56 ERA from 1992–93 as the Mets receded into bottom feeders. But for Doc, rock bottom came in 1994.

He began using cocaine again while injured and received a suspension from MLB. A trip to the Betty Ford Center was no help. Two days after his release, Gooden relapsed. He failed another drug test and was suspended for all of 1995, bringing a sad end to his Mets tenure. The remainder of Gooden's baseball life would be a mixture of comebacks and setbacks as indiscretions got the better of him; he retired in 2001 with a record of 194-112.

Dwight Gooden was perhaps the most gifted player to infiltrate the Mets' universe. Nobody began their career with more promise or possibility. A few pitchers have been able to come near or exceed the numbers he put up, but none had his talent. The demons that played a part in curtailing Gooden's success have never left. Yet he's never handled his troubles with arrogance or defiance, which is why so many are still in his corner.

STARTING PITCHER—JERRY KOOSMAN

Frugality can sometimes have its virtues. Koosman struggled mightily in the minors following a brief Army stint and management was on the verge of releasing the hard-throwing Minnesotan in 1966. Except the front office remembered he owed a sum of less than $100—money borrowed to fund a replacement vehicle after being involved in a small accident with teammates. The Mets kept Koosman pending debt reimbursement.

Nobody knows if he paid them back or not. And eventually, nobody cared.

Within a year, Koosman advanced to Triple-A—adding a curveball to his repertoire. By late 1967, he was promoted to the majors. He had a rough go of it in his nine-start trial period but got an opportunity to join the club when the '68 season began. Before long, it would be the Mets who owed him.

Standing in Tom Seaver's shadow was never a source of discontent. When Koosman concluded his Mets career after 1978, his final stat line was highlighted by 346 starts, 2,544.2 innings pitched, 140 wins, 1,799 strikeouts, 108 complete games, and 26 shutouts. In each of those categories, he was second to the legendary right-hander. But the top left-handed starter in team history may be superior in this regard—as the Mets' greatest big-game pitcher, evidenced most by his performance down the stretch during the magical championship carpet ride of 1969.

Before that season, the Mets took pride in trivial accomplishments—winning a home opener, for instance. And thanks to their rookie southpaw, they did it for the first time ever in their seventh attempt. A complete game shutout of San Francisco came four days after a blanking of the Dodgers in Los Angeles.

Any notion of beginner's luck was dismissed when he stood at 11-2 on June 19—not having allowed more than three runs in any start.

Less than a month later, the 25-year-old protected a 1–0 ninth-inning lead in the All-Star Game at the Astrodome by fanning Carl Yastrzemski. Kooz capped his first full season with 19 victories, 178 K's, and an ERA of 2.08 over 263.2 innings. To many, it merited the NL Rookie of the Year, but not to most. He barely lost out on the honor to future Hall of Famer Johnny Bench. But bigger things—and a greater reward—lay ahead.

There was reason to feel positive going into '69, and the pitching staff was the primary source of that optimism. Seaver, Koosman, Gary Gentry, Nolan Ryan, Tug McGraw, and others gave the impression that they'd be better than before—not that this was a high bar to surpass.

By mid-June, the Mets were at .500—a surprising development for a team typically out of contention by this point. Almost as surprising was that Koosman, too, had a break-even record. His struggles dissipated by summertime as he and the rest of the rotation dealt with a razor-thin margin of error. The Mets offense never put fear into opposing pitchers, averaging less than four runs per contest.

Still, by early September, a miracle was in the making. The Mets had narrowed the distance between them and the Chicago Cubs in the National League East to 2.5 games heading into a Shea showdown. Remarks from Cubs players, dismissive of New York's recent resurgence, fueled the fire of a heated pennant race. Bill Hands, who opposed Koosman in the opener, added kerosene. In the bottom of the first, he threw toward Tommie Agee's head.

"I knew right away I was going to go after their best hitter," Jerry said. "You mess with my hitters, I'm going after your best one. I'll go after him *twice* if I have to!"

He only needed to do it once. Ron Santo's wrist bore the brunt of a Koosman fastball leading off the second inning.

"Kooz proved that he was the warrior I always thought he was," Art Shamsky said. "And everybody on the team respected him for it."

The Cubs soon realized the only effect their intimidation tactic had on the Mets was that it made them tougher. Koosman went the distance as the Mets won 3–2 and closed to within 1.5 games. They'd be in first place two nights later. While New York turned into an unstoppable force down the stretch, beating Koosman also proved to be an impossibility. His start versus the Cubs began a stretch of five consecutive complete games—three of which were shutouts.

He had pitched at such a high level for so long, a letdown seemed inevitable. The Atlanta Braves put a few dents in Koosman's invincible facade in Game 2 of the NLCS. Staked with an 8–0 advantage, Jerry was pelted with a run in the fourth and five in the fifth. The Mets hung on for an 11–8 victory and won two days later to punch their ticket to the World Series, where Koosman would show that the dud in Atlanta was a mere aberration.

Just when it looked like the Mets were drifting down to earth following Tom Seaver's opening game defeat, Koosman kept the Baltimore Orioles' dynamic lineup hitless for six innings. He yielded two hits and a run in the seventh and

Jerry Koosman pitched in Tom Seaver's shadow, but he recorded the two biggest wins in the 1969 World Series. In 2019, the Mets announced that Koosman's No. 36 would be retired, joining Seaver and a select few who have received that honor.
PHOTOFEST

stayed on the mound long enough for the Mets to give him a ninth-inning lead. Koosman would depart one out shy of going the distance, but his effort had swung the momentum back in the Mets' favor. It built further as more outstanding pitching propelled New York to wins in Games 3 and 4 at Shea Stadium. Now one victory from cementing a fairy-tale season for the ages, Gil Hodges called on Koosman to write the final chapter.

Early on, celebratory plans were put on hold. Koosman allowed home runs to the usual—Frank Robinson—and the unusual—opposing pitcher Dave McNally. "They're not getting any more," a frustrated Koosman told his teammates as he stormed into the dugout after the third inning. "Let's go beat 'em!"

True to his word, the Orioles would score no more, limited to just one hit the rest of the way. The Mets, meanwhile, came to life in the sixth, tied the O's in the seventh, and scored the winning margin in the eighth.

As Cleon Jones secured Davey Johnson's flyball on the warning track in left-center field, Koosman jumped into the arms of catcher Jerry Grote as the celebratory masses congregated on the Shea turf. What seemed inconceivable in March came to fruition in October.

This heroic season wasn't without consequences. A tear in Koosman's teres minor muscle put him out for most of May, and bone spurs in his heel nagged him year-round. He pitched through those pains, but a 1970 injury became too painful. While running in the outfield during batting practice in Cincinnati on June 7, Gary Gentry's line drive struck Koosman in the mouth—breaking his upper left jaw and displacing five teeth.

His statistics also took a hit. The decline over the next three years was noticeable, but not drastic. His ERA rose above 3.00 in 1970 and '71 before tilting up to 4.14 in 1972. His complete games took a major slide. And thanks to nagging injuries, his innings totals slipped as well. He also yielded more hits and walks (an average WHIP of 1.254 compared to the 1.080 mark posted during his first two seasons).

The 1973 season elicited a return to form. Koosman's strikeouts still didn't come as frequently, but his stamina was restored—throwing 263 innings and 12 complete games while registering a 2.84 ERA. The Mets also had a little 1969 in them, making a late-season run on the strength of their pitching, which led to another National League pennant. Their rejuvenated left-hander patched together 31.2 scoreless innings from late August into early September, won the penultimate game of the regular season in Chicago, and went all nine innings in Game 3 of the NLCS at Shea Stadium against powerful Cincinnati—though the latter performance didn't get nearly the same attention as the Bud Harrelson–Pete Rose melee and the subsequent antics from unruly Shea fans.

After a rare, short-lived outing in Game 2 of the World Series, Koosman redeemed himself four nights later with the Mets and A's knotted at two wins apiece. His 6.1 innings combined with Tug McGraw's 2.2 innings collectively shut out Oakland, 2–0. Koosman won Game 5—just as he did in 1969. But unlike '69, it left the Mets with one win to get for the title—a win that eluded them as Oakland rallied to take the title on the West Coast.

The World Series defeat lingered through 1974. While the club spent most of the summer languishing in the bottom of the NL East standings, Koosman didn't suffer a significant setback. His 15 wins were the most among Mets starters and his 188 strikeouts were 32 more than the year before. But he allowed 20 more runs in nearly the same number of innings while walking 85. The free passes increased again in 1975—98 over 239.2 innings, which created a career-high 1.385 WHIP. He still posted a winning record at 14-13 to eclipse 100 career victories. But one single-season achievement continued to escape him.

Koosman came one short of 20 wins as early as his rookie year. Stagnant offenses and the absence of some fully healthy seasons prevented him from getting close. But it all came together in 1976. Koosman won in six of his first seven tries, lost five straight, then rattled off 10 victories in 11 decisions. His ERA went from 4.00 at the All-Star break to 2.69 when the year was done. On September 16, Koosman looked the part of a 20-game winner, a label he finally earned on this night. He struck out 13 St. Louis Cardinals, allowing one run on four hits in a complete game gem. Koosman added another victory to his '76 ledger and also attained 200 K's for the first time in his career.

In the estimation of the writers, Koosman polled second to San Diego's Randy Jones for the Cy Young Award, even though Jerry posted a slightly lower ERA, a better winning percentage, and significantly more strikeouts.

It takes a great pitcher to win 20. And in 1977, Koosman proved a great pitcher can also lose 20. In only four of his 32 starts did he allow more than four earned runs. But with an offense that could muster just 3.28 runs per outing, Koosman received the dubious honor of being a 20-game loser subsequent to being a 20-game winner.

If receiving a league low in run support didn't leave Koosman totally disillusioned, then the June departure of Tom Seaver certainly did. The glory days were officially gone. "Tom really was the franchise at that time—and had been," he said. "For them to trade Tom, it was like the worth of the rest of us wasn't that much either. If they were going to trade him, they would probably trade us at the drop of a pin. . . . I didn't see any improvement coming from the Mets organization."

Koosman endured one more season pitching against a stacked deck before demanding a trade to his home state of Minnesota. Wish granted. At age 35, Koosman became a Twin.

And in his debut American League season, he reached 20 victories again. He'd end up with 222 for his 19-year career and likely would've had more if better offenses had backed him up.

But that does nothing to alter the favorable perception Koosman has in the scope of Mets history—admired as the finest left-hander who won the games that mattered most and, thus, remains an indispensable figure of his era.

STARTING PITCHER—JACOB DEGROM

Perhaps no statistic has undergone a greater fall from grace than pitching wins. Once lauded as a measurement for excellence on the mound, its descent into irrelevance has been swift as rotations have expanded, relievers have gained prominence, and starters have become less influential on their own fate. If there were still some hangers-on desperately carrying a torch for the worth of victories before 2018, deGrom's remarkable Cy Young Award performance that year in the face of a 10-9 record extinguished those beliefs. It also cemented him among the ranks of great Mets pitchers.

And in 2019, despite a shaky start, he brought forth similar mound mastery to distinguish himself even further, as he reclaimed the honor of the league's top pitcher for a second year in a row.

To best understand the first season of deGrom's back-to-back reign, it must be put into perspective both in the context of major-league and franchise history. He led all pitchers with a 1.70 ERA—the sixth-lowest since the mound was lowered to its current height in 1969 and the second-best by a starter in this decade. His 269 strikeouts (done over 217 innings) were second in the NL, but his combination of power and precision was a true rarity. Only six pitchers since 1933 have thrown at least 215 innings with an ERA of 1.70 or lower, and deGrom's strikeout total is the highest of that group. His stunning 218 ERA+ placed him among just 36 pitchers who have posted at least a 200 ERA+ since the turn of the 20th century.

His WHIP of 0.912 is the lowest single-season mark by any Met, including Tom Seaver and Dwight Gooden, while both his ERA and ERA+ are second among starters to Gooden's in 1985. DeGrom's FIP (1.98), which was far and away the lowest in the majors, was the best since Gooden's 1984 mark and his 9.6 pitching WAR, according to Baseball-Reference, is the fourth-highest single-season Mets total.

As incredible as deGrom was, the lack of support he got was nothing short of incredible and appalling. A ragged offense and porous bullpen let a bushel of deGrom's tremendous starts go unrewarded. On 11 occasions, he went seven innings and allowed either zero or one run. DeGrom only won three of them. The Mets record in those starts was 12-18.

The ineptitude of those around him made deGrom, who never voiced complaint, even more admirable. Pitching almost every game without a safety net, he allowed three or fewer runs in 29 straight starts—a single-season record—and reeled off 24 successive quality starts (surpassing Seaver's previous team record of 19).

Proving wins is no longer the gold standard for measuring pitching success, deGrom won the Cy Young handily. It was a historic triumph for the pitcher who made it happen and a significant victory for the growing number of new age baseball thinkers.

Not bad for a former shortstop from Stetson University who had barely been mentioned when discussing the hailed crop of young Mets pitchers. In comparison to the quartet of

During Jacob deGrom's back-to-back Cy Young seasons, he compiled a 2.05 ERA, a 0.941 WHIP, and 524 strikeouts.
SHARON CHAPMAN

Matt Harvey, Noah Syndergaard, Zack Wheeler, and Steven Matz, deGrom was in obscurity.

He arrived in the big leagues without the anticipation that would surround Syndergaard in 2015, without the focus that

Long Islander Matz received later that year, and without the hype that engulfed Harvey in 2012 and Wheeler in 2013.

Having not yet developed his complete arsenal of pitches, deGrom was solid but not spectacular in the minors. He had no nickname, he wasn't a local, and he had no desire to bring attention to himself. That still holds true today. He takes the Citi Field mound to Lynyrd Skynyrd's "Simple Man." When it came time to customize the nameplate on the back of his uniform for the annual Players' Weekend, deGrom chose . . . "deGrom."

So in many respects, his unheralded beginning on May 14, 2014, seems appropriate.

Fresh-faced and sporting a shoulder-length mane of hair, it'd be hard for Citi Field security guards to not confuse him with an overzealous teen trying to sneak into the clubhouse. The pressures of making his first start in the Subway Series didn't rattle him. He held the Yankees to one run and four hits over seven innings . . . only to come up on the losing end—a fate which deGrom and Mets fans have become all too familiar with.

After some typical growing pains, deGrom found his groove by July 8. From that point on, he was victorious in eight of nine decisions, struck out 91, and produced an ERA of 1.90.

The solidification of his Rookie of the Year status came in September, when he refused to yield an earned run for 28 consecutive innings. None of the great Mets rookie pitchers—not Seaver, Koosman, Matlack, or Gooden—can claim a string of zeros as impressive. The streak ended on September 15, but that evening at Citi Field began with another splendid sequence. The first eight Miami Marlins deGrom faced struck out, matching the modern-day major-league record and besting the previous franchise mark of six. He wound up with 13 K's over seven innings.

By 2015, deGrom could no longer hide in anonymity. The spotlight shone brighter as the year progressed. The All-Star Game in Cincinnati was Jake's opportunity to prove he was more than just a top rookie. If his goal was to make some of the American League's best hitters look foolish, mission accomplished. Three batters, three swinging strikeouts—all on fastballs clocked near 100 miles per hour and all in a matter of 10 pitches.

The help of a revived offense following a deadline deal for Yoenis Céspedes lifted the Mets into the NL East lead and granted deGrom and the rest of the New York rotation some breathing room. Jake cooled off a bit after a red-hot June and July but ended with the team lead in WAR (5.4) as well as ERA (2.54) and WHIP (0.979) among starters.

As the Mets headed into their first postseason in nine years, deGrom's biggest outings were ahead of him. None was more significant than the deciding contest of the NLDS at Dodger Stadium. It was clear from the beginning that deGrom's best stuff missed the plane to the West Coast. This was nothing close to the same deGrom who notched 13 strikeouts over seven scoreless innings of a Game 1 victory. But what rose to the forefront was a competitive spirit more noteworthy than any such dominance. DeGrom's Game 5 start seemed destined to end very early when he allowed the Dodgers a quick lead, and they were poised to tack on more. But with great composure, he escaped multiple jams to keep the Mets afloat.

"Even when he doesn't have his best stuff or his best command," said David Wright, "he finds a way."

Thanks to Daniel Murphy's home run and some excellent relief work from Noah Syndergaard and Jeurys Familia, deGrom's resolve was rewarded.

He returned five days later to beat the Cubs in Game 3 of an NLCS that became a Mets sweep, but his lone World Series start had the inverse effect of the Division Series clincher. After getting through four innings unscathed, deGrom was pummeled by the Royals in a four-run fifth that led to his departure.

The Mets again qualified for the playoffs in 2016, only the right-hander from DeLand, Florida, wasn't present for the stretch run. His 7-8 record belied a solid 3.04 ERA specifically because of a two-month winless stretch. But there was nothing stopping deGrom on July 17, when he pitched a complete game shutout against the Phillies by allowing just one hit (to the opposing pitcher, no less) and one walk. His game score, a metric devised by Bill James to determine the strength of a starter's outing, was 97—tied for second-best by any Met in a nine-inning contest.

But in the closing weeks, deGrom began to feel numbness in his fingers and discomfort in his elbow. In late September, he opted for season-ending surgery.

Jake avoided the disabled list in 2017. That in itself was an accomplishment. During a disastrous injury-stricken season for the Mets that went beyond the pale, deGrom was one of a handful who survived without a long spell of inactivity. Amid the maelstrom of fallen bodies and disappointing performances, deGrom ended with a record of 15-10 and a 3.53 ERA. And in a rare show of support, he was able to attain victories in eight consecutive starts from June 12 through July 24 to match a franchise mark previously set by Seaver, David Cone, and Bobby Jones. DeGrom got scant notice from the Cy Young electorate that year, then had their full attention the next—when he received all but one first-place vote.

Putting a dazzling exclamation point on a monumental 2018 campaign, in which he retired the final 20 batters he faced, deGrom finished his outing with his 10th strikeout of the night and the 1,000th of his career, making him the fastest Met to reach that milestone.

By 2019, deGrom had the hardware and the contract extension but still didn't have the horseshoe. Jake shook off some early season rust (which ended his record-tying string of quality starts). But before long, vintage deGrom resurfaced. Overcoming more untimely off-nights from his offense, plus a bullpen with more leaks than the *Titanic*, deGrom's 11-8 record and the team's 14-18 mark in games he started wasn't a hindrance to his historical achievement. As the season progressed, and his competition faltered, deGrom climbed up the NL leaderboard in the vital categories for today's MLB: with the highest WAR, the most strikeouts, second-lowest ERA, the second-lowest WHIP, and the third-most innings pitched.

"He's so programmed with everything he does, it's unbelievable," said pitching coach Phil Regan. "He's dedicated, he knows his routine, and he sticks with it."

DeGrom solidified his repeat title with 23 consecutive scoreless frames to end the season, a stellar (yet not surprising) conclusion to a two-year compilation as exceptional as that of any Met who's ever taken the mound. In fact, his stats in that span (2.05 ERA, 524 K's, 0.941 WHIP) compare quite favorably when examining Dwight Gooden (2.00/544/1.013 from 1984 to 1985) and Tom Seaver (2.20/413/1.008 from 1968 to 1969) in their best two-year stretches.

Through six seasons, deGrom was already sixth among Mets in WAR (and the fourth-highest pitcher), fifth in strikeouts, the highest strikeouts per nine innings, second in ERA to Seaver, first in ERA+, and first in WHIP. By every measure he can control, deGrom is firmly placed among the all-time pitching hierarchy. And with the distinct honor of consecutive Cy Youngs, you might say he's in a class all by himself.

STARTING PITCHER—RON DARLING

He was a renaissance man in a profession where many can't spell "renaissance." Darling's cultural eminence was shaped from the outset. Born in Honolulu to a Hawaiian-Chinese mother and a French-Canadian father, the family moved to Millbury, Massachusetts, where he spent most of his childhood. Ron attended Yale, playing football and baseball, then did what every student-athlete does: double major in French and Southeast Asian history.

Darling contradicted the notion of the stereotypical meathead ballplayer. His insight varied from talking literature to discussing an art exhibit to expanding upon the nuances of his split-fingered fastball.

Darling could've succeeded in many fields. Baseball turned out quite well, as he netted the fourth-most wins (when wins had more merit) and seventh-most strikeouts in Mets history. A great mind, great looks, and a great arm. He exuded perfection, which led to teammates mockingly calling him "Mr. P"—a nickname Darling considered derisive.

Ron proved that nobody's perfect as his pitching faults rose to the surface early on. Darling allowed 104 walks in 1984 and a league-worst 114 for 1985. His proclivity for handing out bases on balls was the main source of manager Davey Johnson's frustration and ignited friction that developed between him and Darling for much of their time together.

"Davey and I had a bit of a contentious relationship," Ron said. "There were a lot of father-son aspects to it, but there was an ongoing tension."

The inability of Darling to regularly stay ahead of hitters had Davey reaching for the antacid and he used the press and other players as sounding boards.

"I was the one guy on our staff he would single out and criticize in a public way," Darling said. "So he dished, usually in a once-removed way, to reporters or teammates. His style was to make sure his comments got back to me, but he rarely put them to me directly."

A probable cause for Johnson's angst might've been that Darling's development paled in comparison to fellow rookie Dwight Gooden, who dispensed with any learning curve and took on a direct upward trajectory. While Doc made instant headway toward pitching stardom, Darling—who had arrived in the Mets system through a trade with the Rangers two years earlier—rammed into roadblocks. He struggled to get on track at the beginning of 1984 after pitching decently as a callup late in 1983. But June began a stretch in which Darling won seven straight and finished the year with a respectable 12-9 record and a 3.81 ERA.

His 16-5 mark and 2.90 ERA with 167 strikeouts plus an All-Star nod in 1985 appeared pedestrian in the shadow of Gooden's Cy Young domination. But Darling commanded the attention on October 1. Down three games in the NL East to St. Louis with six to play, and facing the Cardinals at Busch Stadium, the Mets could ill-afford another loss. Saddled with the most pressure in his young career, Darling matched John Tudor through nine scoreless frames. The Mets prevailed that night but ultimately lost out on the division title. Not next year.

As New York bolstered their rotation with the addition of Bob Ojeda along with the emergence of Sid Fernandez, Darling sharpened the effectiveness of his splitter—the revolutionary

With more brain power than most athletes, Ron Darling won 99 games primarily utilizing his split-fingered fastball.

pitch of the decade—while marshaling his control. The end results were a career-high 184 strikeouts and only 81 walks. Although he had one fewer victory than the previous year (while still losing six), the Mets were 26-8 in games he started and won in 11 of his 13 no-decisions.

As part of a pitching staff that led the league in ERA and a team that was markedly better than the competition, Darling realized the perks that came with success in New York—gracing magazine covers and talk shows—while also experiencing the drawbacks—like when he and three teammates were arrested in Houston following a brawl with undercover cops.

But the benefits far outweighed any downsides. Darling made his postseason debut in Game 3 of the NLCS. A dream scenario turned nightmarish almost instantly. The visiting Astros tagged Darling for four runs before he could escape the second inning. Relieved by Rick Aguilera on the mound and Darryl Strawberry at the plate, Darling was granted a reprieve. The Mets right fielder cranked a tying three-run homer in the sixth inning that got his starter off the hook. New York won on Lenny Dykstra's walk-off blast and split the next two to bring the series back to Houston.

Game 6's outcome would determine Darling's upcoming start. Because the Mets outlasted the Astros in a 16-inning classic, he bypassed a winner-take-all showdown against Mike Scott at the Astrodome and instead was entrenched in a World Series opening duel at Shea with Bruce Hurst.

Darling embarked on 15 straight innings without permitting the Red Sox an earned run. But betrayed by a lack of offensive support and a costly error by Tim Teufel, he ended up the hard-luck loser of Game 1. Ron kept the Sox off the scoreboard for seven innings in Game 4 at Fenway Park. Just miles from the town where he grew up, the Millbury native helped even the series at two. Another remarkable Game 6 rally and a rainout gave Darling the task of starting Game 7 on four days' rest. He was matched again with Hurst, but Darling was unable to meet the challenge. Davey Johnson's short leash had Darling depart on the short end of a 3–0 Boston lead. Never would a no-decision feel so good.

He would ultimately be bailed out by Sid Fernandez, who threw 2.1 hitless innings; Keith Hernandez, who drove in two runs with a sixth-inning single; and Ray Knight, the series MVP, who cracked the game-winning homer in the seventh.

"Because my teammates found a way to rally and get me off the hook and grab that championship trophy, every member of that 1986 New York Mets team holds a special place in the hearts and minds of our great fans—myself included," Darling wrote in his 2016 book.

After reaping the added spoils of a championship in the Big Apple, he then experienced the hardships that come with trying to maintain that level of performance. When Dwight Gooden was forced to miss the first two months of the 1987 regular season because of a positive cocaine test, coupled with an injury to Bob Ojeda, Darling became the de facto ace. Unfortunately, the reliability Darling conveyed with regularity in 1986 went missing in early '87 as he was 2-4 with a 5.58 ERA in the 12 starts during Gooden's absence. After Doc returned in early June, Darling went 10-4 with a 3.62 ERA, at one point winning six straight and taking 11 of his final 14 starts. Darling avoided the injury bug until September, when torn ligaments in his right thumb kept him from helping New York down the stretch.

The Darling of 1988, however, more closely resembled the Darling of 1986. In some cases, he was better. Constant aggravation from bone chips in his right elbow couldn't stop him from a career-high 17 wins and his best strikeout-to-walk ratio. Twenty-four of his 34 starts lasted at least seven innings, including a complete game on September 22 that clinched another division title.

On an unseasonably cold and uncomfortably wet early October Saturday afternoon at Shea with the Mets and Los Angeles Dodgers knotted at one win apiece, Darling braved the elements and came away with a final line of three runs allowed over six innings. While he didn't factor in the Mets' late victory, Darling believed the decision to suit up was questionable at best.

"Worst day I've ever played baseball in," he said afterward in the locker room. "Should've never played."

He probably wished that would've happened in his next start. The Game 7 reprieve he got two years ago at Shea was not to be at Dodger Stadium. Darling was the victim of a collective Mets meltdown in the second inning. Two errors and a misplayed bunt paved the way to five L.A. runs. Darling was done early. So were the Mets, whose bats were silenced by Orel Hershiser's brilliance.

Misfortune seeped into 1989. He began 0-3 with an 8.20 ERA over his first four starts. While Darling regressed in nearly every category, his steady fielding warranted a Gold Glove Award. No Mets pitcher had received it before, and none has won it since. He also managed 14 victories, and joined Tom Seaver as the only other Met to win at least 10 games in six straight seasons.

The depth of the starting staff was evident in the fact that Darling, despite still being worthy of inclusion, was battling

Ojeda for the fifth spot in the rotation behind Gooden, ex–Minnesota Twin Frank Viola, David Cone, and Fernandez.

As the 1990 season panned out, neither Darling nor Ojeda stood out. Darling got 18 starts, won seven, lost nine and suffered the worst WHIP of his career at 1.42. A modest recovery was enough to give him the upper hand in 1991. Through July 14, he had started 17 times and was able to bring his career win total to 99.

But at that time, the Mets' needs centered on securing a setup man, and they felt they had found one in Montreal. Darling turned out to be the expendable piece sent to the Expos in exchange for Tim Burke. But Ron's stay north of the border was brief. Within 16 days, Darling moved again—this time to Oakland, where he was second on the club in wins in 1992 and made one more postseason appearance. By 1995, Darling was out of baseball. He had an inclination of where he'd end up eventually, preferably lending his depth of knowledge to a front office role.

"Maybe somewhere down the road I'll do that with my alma mater, the Mets," he said in 2001.

Five years later, Darling would prove himself right—only in a different capacity. Alongside Keith Hernandez and Gary Cohen, Darling has formed a broadcast team on SNY that's equal parts insightful and entertaining and has heightened his status as a Mets fan favorite.

STARTING PITCHER—JON MATLACK

If Jacob deGrom is the modern Mets example of pitching proficiency gone unfulfilled by wins, he may as well be following in the footsteps of the lanky left-hander. Even though Matlack pitched back when starters went deeper and relievers were more infrequently utilized, his quality work was often done in by pedestrian Met hitting. There's no better source for historical context than 1974.

That year, he ended with a 2.41 ERA—good enough for third in the National League. Among pitchers, he led the league in WAR at 9.1. His seven shutouts also paced the NL, and Matlack finished in the top 10 in innings pitched, WHIP, strikeouts, and strikeout-to-walk ratio. And what did he get for all his trouble? A 13-15 record. That's because too often he was left to fend for himself.

In his season debut, Matlack surrendered just one run to the Phillies in seven-plus innings of a 9–2 Mets victory. He should've savored this abundance of help—because that would be the only time in 1974 when the Mets scored more than six runs for him. When the season was done, New York's anemic offense averaged a mere 3.15 runs in Matlack's outings.

But the limited support was nothing relative to the absence of consolation from Cy Young Award voters. In a time when dinosaur writers roamed the baseball landscape and sabermetrics had not yet permeated the baseball vernacular, wins and losses carried tremendous weight in determining the best pitcher.

Unfairly, Matlack was not among the 11 who garnered NL Cy Young votes, most of whom were granted at least a full run more of support than the shortchanged Mets lefty. That '74 season served as an exaggerated symbol of his six-year stint in New York. He won 82; he lost 81. An almost break-even record—and a severely misleading mark, too.

From his stellar rookie campaign in 1972 through 1976, Matlack racked up 23 shutouts with a 2.84 ERA. For the sake of comparison, Tom Seaver racked up 21 shutouts with a 2.61 ERA and won 87 times during that same span. Jerry Koosman's ERA was 3.22 with 11 shutouts and 75 wins. Matlack certainly didn't measure up to Seaver and Koosman, but the disparity between them, specifically in that five-year window, wasn't all that significant.

Matlack often was regarded as second or third fiddle on a staff with a first-ballot Hall of Famer and a fellow southpaw already boasting the reputation of being one of the elite left-handers. But he did get his fair share of deserved attention soon after entering the majors. A career-low 2.32 ERA, a career-high 205 strikeouts, and a 1.172 WHIP during a 15-victory season distinguished him as the second Met ever to be named Rookie of the Year in 1972 while learning from pitchers who similarly dazzled during their formative days. "The fact that my locker was between [the lockers of] Seaver and Koosman says enough," he said.

Following a handful of provisional starts in 1971, Matlack put his knowledge to work right away in '72, notching his first win on April 23 against Chicago by allowing one hit over four innings in relief of Gary Gentry. Five days later in Los Angeles, Jon got a chance to finish what he started. The Dodgers could only manage a run on six hits. This was the first of eight complete games—a nice way to ensure job security.

It would be June before Matlack tasted defeat. His 15 wins and 205 strikeouts were slightly behind Seaver for the team lead; but in the categories of WAR (6.0), shutouts (four), and ERA (2.32), he stood a cut above. The pupil had outshone the instructors.

But that shine wore off quickly. Matlack began to fall into the dreaded sophomore slump—starting off 1973 by allowing at least four runs in three of his first six outings, something he did just five times for all of 1972.

Then on May 8, a dreary and drizzly evening in front of a paltry 6,840 at Shea, more than just his career flashed before him. A searing line drive came off the bat of Atlanta's Marty Perez and headed right back where it came from—a pitcher's worst fear. The ball nicked Matlack's glove and struck him square on the left side of his forehead. The ricochet actually allowed two Braves runners to score, but that concern was mild compared to the pressing worry about the condition of the 23-year-old pitching star as he writhed on the mound. Both teams gathered around Matlack before he was placed on a stretcher and hauled away to a local hospital. The final diagnosis was a fractured skull. And in what can only be deemed a baseball miracle, Matlack returned to the same mound 11 days later, wearing a hockey goalie's headband for protection.

The 1972 Rookie of the Year, Jon Matlack finished his Mets career with a 3.03 ERA.
COURTESY OF JON MATLACK

If he appeared timid in the wake of his brush with mortality, it would have been understandable. But Matlack soon shook off any residual fears and regained the form of his rookie year at a very opportune time.

On his way to ranking third in the National League in strikeouts with 205, Jon won six of his final seven regular-season decisions, most coming during a stretch in which New York went 24-9 to go from worst to first in the NL East.

Matlack's hot hand carried into October, as his smooth delivery held postseason opponents to four runs over 25.2 innings. Game 2 of the NLCS marked his finest performance—at a juncture when the Mets were desperate to regain momentum from the Cincinnati Reds.

New York wasn't facing a must-win situation by the ordinary standards, but there was a sense of urgency when considering who it was up against—a lineup of Hall of Fame–worthy bats: Pete Rose, Joe Morgan, Tony Pérez, and Johnny Bench. This was as close as you could get to a 1970s version of "Murderer's Row."

Keeping them in check would be a task far easier said than done. Tom Seaver almost did it, only to be victimized by solo homers from Rose and Bench in a tough-luck 2–1 opening game defeat.

Matlack, meanwhile, negotiated the explosive Reds attack and barely permitted them to reach base. Forgoing his usual volume of fastballs, he instead relied on an assortment of breaking pitches to throw Cincinnati's power hitters off-balance. It worked to near perfection. In a 5–0 victory, the only two hits charged to Matlack came from unheralded Andy Kosco. As for the powerful heart of the order, the quartet of Rose, Morgan, Pérez, and Bench combined to go 0-for-16.

Little changed for the rest of the series. The Reds mustered just six runs. Game 5's 7–2 win ended with Matlack in the bullpen—in case Tug McGraw encountered ninth-inning trouble. Rather than an emergency role in the fifth game, he got the starting assignment for the opener of the World Series.

Since this series went seven games, Matlack got three starts—each against Oakland's Ken Holtzman. He won just once, but he didn't allow an earned run in two of those outings. Victimized in Game 1 on a grounder under the legs of normally reliable second baseman Félix Millán, which led to a 2–1 loss, Matlack came back stronger in Game 4—going eight innings and yielding three hits in a 6–1 New York victory that drew the Mets even with the A's. Matlack was asked to pitch the seventh game on three days' rest. It was his lone postseason stumble. The costliest missteps came in the third inning. Two-run blasts from Bert Campaneris and eventual series MVP Reggie Jackson knocked out Matlack and the Mets staggered to a state from which they wouldn't recover.

Jon didn't lose his touch—or his patience—in 1974, even though his team appeared punch-drunk year-round. His season finale proved quite symbolic. In a 10-inning affair with the Phillies, Matlack went the whole way, allowing just one earned run and walking three. And he lost.

Most of the public ignored Matlack's excellence in the face of misfortune, but he was recognized by those who knew him best. Yogi Berra, by virtue of being the manager for the defending pennant winners, was in charge of filling out the National League All-Star roster of pitchers and reserves and chose Matlack. He pitched a scoreless inning in what would be the first of three consecutive Midsummer Classic appearances. The next year, in Milwaukee, Matlack's two shutout frames along with five strikeouts earned him a win and a share of the MVP award with Bill Madlock. As for the games that counted, he experienced better results in his win-loss mark (16-12), even as his ERA (3.38) and his strikeout total (154) didn't show improvement.

In 1976, he got great results, an offense to back him up, and a hint of respect from the baseball writers. Matlack wound up sixth in the Cy Young Award balloting. He won 17 games and lost 10 with a league-best six shutouts and an ERA under 3.00 for the third time in five years (2.95 to be exact).

Unfortunately, his final season in New York was his worst, almost counteracting the great success from '76. Laboring through a year of seven victories and 15 defeats, Jon had his lowest strikeout total (123), his highest home run allowance rate (one per nine innings), and his highest WHIP (1.290). The most alarming increase was his ERA—a career-worst 4.21.

Nevertheless, when Matlack ventured to Texas post-1977—where he'd play for the duration of his 13-year big-league career—his 3.03 ERA was second-best to Seaver among pitchers who had recorded at least 700 innings in a Mets uniform. More than 40 years later, it still is.

STARTING PITCHER—AL LEITER

Whether good or bad, you always knew his feelings in real-time. Leiter wore emotions on his sleeve—and just about anywhere else he could. He would've made a terrible poker player, but the left-hander from Toms River, New Jersey, emitted an infectious passion that the Mets fed off of during the late 1990s and early 2000s.

New York took advantage of a Florida Marlins' post–World Series fire sale, and it paid immediate dividends. After pitching for the Fish in the postseason, including the deciding game of the '97 Fall Classic, it was apparent that Leiter wasn't about to be deterred by the pressures of New York. It came to fruition right away.

In a year when home runs were flying out at a record pace, Leiter gave up only eight. When the median ERA of all major-league pitchers was a hefty 4.42, Leiter's was a robust 2.47. And in a season in which the collective league-wide batting average was .266, Leiter held opposing hitters to .216. He also led all Mets in victories with 17 while losing just six and walked 71 batters two years after he led the NL with 119 free passes.

This earned Leiter a contract extension worth four years and $32 million—part of an offseason spending spree (which included retaining Mike Piazza and acquiring Robin Ventura) indicative of the Mets' insistence on ending their 11-year postseason drought.

But even as the Mets took on the look of a contender in 1999, Leiter was not living up to his new price tag. The consistency he once exhibited had gone astray. Through May, Leiter's ERA soared north of 6.00. Even though he'd rebound in June, his reliability dissipated. That would change by late September.

In the waning days of the regular season, it seemed as if New York wouldn't be playing past the scheduled finale. The Mets' playoff chances went from likely to doubtful in a matter of a week. They managed to recover from a seven-game freefall when Leiter outdueled Greg Maddux on September 29 and later forced a one-game playoff with the Cincinnati Reds that would sort out the NL Wild Card. It gave the Mets a chance to avoid the humiliation of a second consecutive late-season tailspin. And on a personal note, it offered an opportunity for Leiter to balance out what had been an uneven six months.

Looking every bit like the ace pitcher the Mets hoped he'd be, Leiter finessed a brilliant two-hit complete game shutout that gave New York its first postseason berth since 1988.

"Al has pitched a no-hitter," Bobby Valentine said, referring to a night in 1996 with Florida. "But I don't know if he's ever pitched a better game."

The drama that typically encompasses a winner-take-all affair lessened when Edgardo Alfonzo went deep with a two-run homer in the top of the first. Leiter's dominance on the mound proceeded to eliminate any tension—and eventually the Reds as well.

Leiter overcame a wobbly beginning in which he allowed a baserunner in each of first three innings, at one point retiring 13 Reds in a row. He dotted the strike zone beautifully with pitches that led to seven strikeouts and rarely resulted in hard contact.

"I felt like I was leading by 10 runs, once I settled in," he said. "I had a good curveball that night."

A ninth-inning Cincinnati threat was merely an effort to try and end the shutout. After a leadoff double, the Reds couldn't even do that. The last batted ball, off the lumber of Dimitri Young, lined directly into the glove of Alfonzo to put the finishing touch on a 5–0 masterpiece.

Behind the finest night in the career of its gritty left-hander, New York dispatched Cincinnati and departed for Arizona to prolong its October thrill ride. The Mets took two of the first three versus the Diamondbacks before Leiter took the mound again. Game 4 of the NLDS at Shea was his second straight opportunity to extend a New York season that had seemed hopeless just a week earlier. Leiter set down the first 13 D-Backs in order and left in the eighth with a 2–1 lead. That quickly evaporated as Armando Benítez allowed a two-run double but was salvaged by the thrilling conclusion created from Todd Pratt's series-ending walk-off homer.

Game 3 of the NLCS versus Atlanta furthered Leiter's reputation as a big-game pitcher yet deepened the Mets' frustration. The Braves could only muster three hits and one run—a run that came off mistakes from the New York battery. First-inning throwing errors by Leiter and Mike Piazza provided Atlanta the scoring it needed as the Mets bats fell silent. Leiter was valiant in a hard-luck defeat, but nothing could dignify his Game 6 performance.

New York had flirted with elimination and escaped exile twice—the latter a 15-inning Game 5 victory which required Valentine to expend every one of his fresh arms. On three days' rest, a condition that had never been favorable to him before, it was imperative for Leiter to keep the Braves down while simultaneously preventing the bullpen from being overworked.

The end result was a total mess. Leiter suffered through a miserable first inning—one he couldn't get out of before Valentine gave a quick hook. After 25 pitches, Leiter had as many hit batters as hits allowed (two) and was responsible for five Braves runs—all without recording an out. The Mets actually managed to bail out their beleaguered lefty until bowing out in the 11th.

Leiter came back in 2000 a far more consistent pitcher than he was in '99. He lowered his ERA by almost a full run, went 16-8, made his second All-Star appearance, and reached the 200-strikeout plateau for the second time.

Neither the Mets nor Leiter would have to endure a one-game playoff. Instead, he was needed to help even the Division

Al Leiter's stats are misleading because of the era in which he pitched, but he was the best starter in the late 1990s and early 2000s.
JERRY COLI/DREAMSTIME

Series with San Francisco and avoid an 0-2 series hole. Even after surrendering a double to Barry Bonds to lead off the ninth, Leiter had New York in a position to do just that. But as he would discover several times this postseason, wins were hard to come by. A single and a homer handed Leiter the cruel fate of a no-decision, but the Mets eventually found a way to depart the Bay Area with a split.

New York dispensed with the Giants, meaning Al's next start came in Game 2 of the NLCS at Busch Stadium. He wasn't as sharp yet had the same end result: a New York victory, but not a Leiter victory.

The Mets kept on winning to set up an all–New York World Series. While emotions were high in the city and among the two ballclubs, they were especially poignant for Leiter, the Game 1 starter who began his career in the Yankee organization. He got through seven innings with two runs, three walks, seven strikeouts, and the lead. But the advantage he so staunchly protected didn't hold for long, as Benítez let another get away.

Logic dictates if the Mets had won Game 1, they wouldn't have lost the series in Game 5. Perhaps, but what is certain is that Yankee resolve withstood Leiter's tenacity. In what might have been his most high-profile showcase of determination, he suffered one of his most agonizing defeats.

Leiter strove to single-handedly fend off a Yankee three-peat, even instigating a run-scoring play with a perfectly placed bunt. As his pitch count crept toward a season-high 142, successive two-out ninth-inning hits against the exhausted lefty plated two tie-breaking runs and spoiled hopes of sending the Subway Series back to the Bronx. It also brought a haunting nightmare to life: the hated rivals celebrating a championship on Shea Stadium grounds.

Over the next four seasons, 2001–04, Leiter averaged 30 starts and maintained a 3.50 ERA but no longer enjoyed the same success he had during the playoff runs. Consequently, the Mets drifted further away from postseason contention each year. By the end of 2004, Leiter ranked high on some Mets all-time lists: sixth in wins (95) and seventh in strikeouts (1,106).

As his career neared its conclusion, the Mets were in a transition phase themselves. Leiter became one of the casualties of the rebuilding effort and was declined a $10 million option for 2005, leaving a somewhat bitter taste that was soothed when he returned to the organization as special advisor in 2018.

While the numbers Leiter accumulated over seven seasons don't measure up to the other great starting pitchers, they are impressive when considering the period in which he performed. It's difficult to judge him against those who were afforded the luxury of pitching in less hitter-friendly eras. A few advanced statistical measures, though, make it clearer.

Leiter's overall Mets ERA is not among the top 10 in franchise history, but his 124 ERA+ is. His pitching WAR of 28.0 is fifth among all Met arms. And as for his adjusted pitching runs, used to measure the number of runs prevented from scoring compared to the league's average pitcher in a neutral park, Leiter remains fourth—trailing only Tom Seaver, Jacob deGrom, and Dwight Gooden.

RELIEF PITCHER—TUG McGRAW

In July 1973, McGraw's career approached a crossroads. His ERA through 41.9 innings that season was a sizable 6.20. He had nearly as many blown saves as converted saves. His team, too, was at a breaking point. Following a July 7 game in which McGraw reliquished a late lead against Atlanta, the Mets dropped to 34-45 and 12.5 games back in the NL East.

As local newspapers polled fans on who should take the fall, team chairman M. Donald Grant held a clubhouse meeting in which he emphasized his faith in the Mets to turn matters around. During this collective vote of confidence, McGraw belted out the phrase that would become this team's trademark. Many Mets players laughed off his "Ya Gotta Believe" rallying cry as nothing more than typical behavior from their left-handed free spirit. Grant wasn't so amused. He told McGraw later that his job was on the line. Tug eventually turned his own words into action, and the rest of the Mets would subsequently turn McGraw into a prophet.

New York's climb from last place in late August to the National League pennant in October paralleled his own revival. Over the last six weeks of the regular season, Tug made 19 appearances, saved 12, won five, and had a razor-thin ERA of 0.88. In the Mets' final 25 victories, which allowed them to take the NL East by 1.5 games, McGraw factored in 17 of them. He also finished off the NLCS clincher as well as two key World Series victories.

No player better epitomized, closely mirrored, and is more strongly associated with the 1973 Mets season than McGraw. But there's more than three words or three months to his Mets legacy.

McGraw emerged from early struggles to become the workhorse of the bullpen and protect the lucrative win totals of Seaver, Koosman, and Gary Gentry with a 2.24 ERA and a 9-3 record for the 1969 champions.

After a step back in 1970, McGraw put forth the best year for any Mets reliever. Sharing fireman duties with Danny Frisella limited Tug to eight saves, but he went 11-4 in 1971 with an ERA of 1.70 while holding batters to a .189 average.

McGraw duplicated that 1.70 ERA in 1972, and now was getting more recognition. New manager Yogi Berra used McGraw almost twice as often as Frisella, and he racked up

Tug McGraw epitomized the 1973 Mets' charge to the National League pennant.
PHOTOFEST

27 saves—which stood as a club record for 12 years. Tug also made a key appearance in the All-Star Game and picked up the extra-inning victory in Atlanta. McGraw struck out three in the ninth and fanned four over two innings.

Tug brought respect and admiration to a role that didn't invoke much esteem at that time. He also possessed an ideal mental makeup—an optimistic bohemian with a great sense of humor and the good sense to keep a short-term memory, never letting what happened in the prior outing, good or bad, affect the next one. Merging aptitude and attitude along with a boyish look and boyish enthusiasm, he grew into a crowd favorite. But no pitcher, especially one vying for major-league attention, has his initial sights set on being a reliever. Tug wasn't any different.

The Mets discovered him purely by chance. Scout Roy Partee had his eye on older brother Hank, a catching prospect, and signed him for $15,000. But Tug's slow curveball garnered notice, and he was eventually inked for $7,000. The return on investment for Tug made the money spent on Hank, who never amounted to much, worthwhile.

McGraw made a favorable impression by outpitching Sandy Koufax at a time when not many others could do so. Tug's 7.2 superb innings ensured Koufax's 13-game win streak against the Mets would end. But quality outings for McGraw came few and far between.

After 1966, he was demoted to the instructional league. It was there that Tug began implementing the screwball, a pitch which darts in on left-handed batters and away from righties. This would ultimately change his career, but his turnaround took a while.

McGraw made four forgettable starts at the tail end of 1967, enough to keep him in the minors through 1968. When he vied for another major-league opportunity the next spring training, it was under the direction of new manager Gil Hodges—an opposite to Tug in every way except the shared experience of Marine Corps service.

McGraw pitched well enough in the spring to earn a spot on the Opening Day roster, just not as a starter. Hodges felt

McGraw was better suited to complement veteran right-hander Ron Taylor out of the bullpen. Like many of Gil's decisions that year, it worked to brilliant effect.

Hodges's newest reliever made 38 appearances over 79.2 innings. Tug won eight times and saved 12 with a 1.47 ERA. From July 31 through October 1, a 38-inning span, McGraw allowed two earned runs.

As integral as he was to the Mets' advance to the NL East crown, Tug was limited during the playoffs and especially so in the World Series, when Mets starters recorded all but eight outs in Games 2 through 5. Tug's lone postseason outing in 1969, though, fortified his confidence.

It came in Game 2 of the NLCS in Atlanta. McGraw was asked to stave off a potential Braves' comeback and keep the Mets' lead intact. He responded with three shutout innings and earned the save in the 11–6 victory that gave New York a two-game edge in the best-of-five series.

"Thanks to that NLCS appearance, I was convinced that I was not only a viable major leaguer, but one who could excel in the future," he later wrote in his autobiography. "Everything changed for me in 1969, the year we turned out to be god-damned amazing, all right."

Four years later, Tug would be back in the World Series after another test of personal conviction. He began 1973 with a 1.32 ERA and five saves through May 3, then reversed course—blowing seven of 13 save chances and allowing 32 runs in 33 innings. The Mets tried to get McGraw out of his massive funk by moving him into the starting rotation. That failed, too. But Tug's positive thinking and his proven abilities led him to regain his talents and lift a floundering team ravaged by injuries.

New York benefited from the mediocrity of its divisional competition and the timely return of many key players. The Mets remained in the cellar in late August, 6.5 games out, before making their ascent.

Tug was never better than at the end. Beginning on August 22 (when he still had a 5.45 ERA), he allowed just four earned runs over the next 41 innings. He notched 12 crucial saves, including the one at foggy Wrigley Field on October 1 that brought this unusual NL East race to a close.

McGraw temporarily took a backseat to the starters in the NLCS against Cincinnati, as Seaver, Jon Matlack, and Koosman each went the distance in their respective outings. His workload increased significantly by Game 4. He worked 4.1 scoreless—but stressful—innings, tiptoeing out of jams in the eighth and ninth and aided in the 11th by Rusty Staub's spectacular catch. The 1–1 deadlock held until Harry Parker surrendered a Pete Rose homer in the 12th. The Mets' attempt to claim the NL pennant was delayed for only a day.

Just as he did in the division clincher, Tug spelled Seaver, this time with the bases full and the Mets holding a 7–2 ninth-inning advantage. After a pop out, McGraw induced a grounder from Dan Driessen. He ran over to cover first base, took the toss from John Milner, and touched the bag just as a rabid sea of humanity engulfed Shea. The frenzy that followed the final out symbolized the frantic ride the Mets had taken for six months, with McGraw in the front car of the roller-coaster.

Contrary to his invisibility in the '69 Fall Classic, McGraw logged 13.2 innings during the '73 series. Almost half his work was done in Game 2—the longest World Series contest to date. When he took over in the seventh, the Mets held a 6–3 lead.

That advantage would evaporate by the ninth, as Willie Mays's infamous stumble in center field paved the way for the tying runs.

He remained on the Oakland Coliseum mound into the 12th in a circumstance reserved for baseball's stone age. McGraw had a more conventional two-inning, one-hit, no-run outing in Game 3 at Shea, earned a one-night breather, then got the final eight outs to save a 2–0 Game 5 victory. The Mets were a win from scaling the base of a mountain to the summit in a matter of two months. But they wouldn't get to the summit. The Mets lost both in Oakland, with a brief McGraw appearance in Game 6 to solidify a 1.93 ERA over 13.2 postseason innings.

Opening Day 1974 was an omen for McGraw and the Mets. Tug allowed a game-winning homer to Mike Schmidt in Philadelphia. With the magic of late '73 in absentia, New York lost 91 times. Tug's ERA rose to 4.16, and he had his lowest K/9 rate and his highest HR/9 figure since becoming a full-time reliever.

By the end of the year, New York was in fifth place and McGraw was about to be in Philadelphia. The Mets never considered that Tug's tired shoulder could be mended by a quick fix. Considered damaged goods, he was shipped (along with two others) to their divisional rivals for a trio that included John Stearns. After the trade, it was revealed that Tug had a simple cyst that required minor surgery.

McGraw departed as the Mets leader in saves, games pitched, and games finished. He would be part of four Phillies playoff teams and the bullpen ace that helped bring them their first World Series title in 1980.

It's almost impossible for an athlete in a team sport to gain adulation from New York *and* Philadelphia. McGraw, though, was the rare breed who could do it. A reservoir of abundant zest, Tug's magnetic personality was plainly evident. Even as he battled and ultimately succumbed to cancer in 2004, McGraw's belief was as strong then as it had been nearly three decades earlier.

Relief Pitcher—John Franco

Many young kids aspire to be major leaguers. Few get to achieve it. Fewer get to achieve it playing with the team they grew up rooting for. Franco, a Brooklyn native and alum of St. John's University, is in that select group.

The dream scenario didn't pan out right away. From St. John's, Franco was drafted by the Dodgers, who then dealt him to the Reds, where he spent six seasons compiling 148 of the 424 saves he'd accumulate over his 21-year big-league career.

When the Mets sent their left-handed reliever Randy Myers in exchange for Cincinnati's, Franco was coming home—to play in the stadium where he cheered the Mets to World Series glory in 1969 and pitch on the same mound as his favorite, Tug McGraw. He'd stay for 15 years, racking up personal milestones and team records, while becoming a major-league record holder as the most successful left-handed closer.

"You have to have some thick skin to play (in New York)," Franco said. "It's hard. Especially as a relief pitcher, you have to be able to turn the page quite a bit. Some guys could handle it, some couldn't."

John spoke from firsthand experience. But he didn't make it easy on Mets fans. Franco piled up a franchise-best 276 saves. From this pleasure came occasional pain. Watching Franco execute saves was often an exercise in frustration. He never embodied the identity of a shutdown reliever. He was more of an escape artist, often walking the proverbial high wire thanks to a higher WHIP than his closer contemporaries. But that angst usually led to satisfaction. He converted 81 percent of his save opportunities.

Comfortable with familiar surroundings in 1990, Franco led the NL and established a new Mets single-season save record with 33 as the reliance on closers gained traction. He likely would have broken his own mark in 1994. Franco was atop the league again with 30 before the players' strike brought the season to its knees. This began a four-year stretch in which he averaged 33 saves and never finished with an ERA worse than 2.70.

The relievers portion of the Mets record book would be rewritten by Franco as his career played out. In early 1996, he crossed off a personal milestone that had been done by just seven others: save number 300.

"This one," Franco said afterward, "was for all the doubters." Those doubts sprouted from fans and critics alike, who were especially vocal when he began the year squandering three of his initial five save chances.

Franco regained form for the most part, posting his lowest ERA since 1992 and surrendering just two home runs in 54 innings. But while he saved 28 games, a source of concern arose in his difficulty in putting out fires. John inherited 20 runners in '96—12 of whom came around to score. The Mets brass briefly considered replacing Franco with an up-and-coming reliever. But management remained loyal to their local lefty, and John upheld allegiance to his hometown club.

"I feel I could have gotten more on the open market," he said. "There have been hard times. But if I win, I want to win here."

Franco's loyalty was rewarded starting in 1997. The Mets made significant progress under manager Bobby Valentine's

Brooklyn native John Franco became the all-time save leader among left-handers while playing for his hometown team.

leadership. John's save total reflected that. With more opportunities to lock down wins, he saved 74 over the next two seasons.

He also welcomed new teammates who could enhance his chances of a first postseason trip. Franco voluntarily passed off his No. 31 to Mike Piazza when the slugging catcher arrived to New York in May 1998 and offered him a guest room in his house to give the newest Met acquisition time to find a place in his new city.

But as the Mets were turning into a legitimate National League contender, Franco began to show some vulnerability. He allowed the most hits and the most runs since his out-of-character struggles of 1993. Although he saved 38 and was inducing strikeouts at a greater rate than ever before, this gave reason for some to speculate that the 37-year-old needed a demotion. Franco would indeed relinquish his closer duties—but not because of a managerial decision.

It developed into a bittersweet 1999 for Franco. He began by converting his first 14 save opportunities, including the one in mid-April versus the Florida Marlins that made him just the second pitcher in history to reach 400 saves.

"It's amazing," Franco said afterward. "But now I'd like to go on to the next level and make it to the postseason. Hopefully, this will be the year."

Franco's wish would be fulfilled, but not without distress. A partial tear to the flexor tendon of his left middle finger in early July took him out of action until early September. His departure ceded the closer responsibilities to Armando Benítez, a job he wouldn't surrender.

Now relegated to setup man, Franco responded with 12.3 consecutive scoreless innings, which stretched through the regular season, the NLDS triumph over Arizona, and into the NLCS with Atlanta. He finally relinquished an earned run at a rather inopportune moment. With the Mets clinging to a one-run lead in the eighth inning of Game 6 following a frantic comeback, Franco surrendered a one-out RBI single that retied the score. New York fought valiantly but fell in 11 innings—two wins short of Franco's first World Series.

He'd only have to wait another year for that Fall Classic appearance. The Mets again made their way to the postseason via the wild card in 2000, while Franco kept a secondary role to Benítez in the bullpen. There was no reason for manager Valentine to consider a switch back. Benítez saved 41 games and averaged 12.3 K's per nine innings. Meanwhile, over 64 appearances, Franco's ERA was an uncharacteristic 3.40—still second-lowest among Mets relievers.

For Franco and Benítez, Game 2 of the NLDS would see their roles reversed, but it was certainly not by choice. After dropping the opener in San Francisco, a second straight loss would put the Mets in, shall we say, Giant trouble.

Benítez's attempt to stymie the NL West champs dissolved on the heels of J. T. Snow's three-run homer down the right-field line. The Mets regained the lead in the tenth, then Franco was called upon to get the final three outs after Benítez allowed a leadoff single.

With the tying run on, two outs, and Barry Bonds up, it served as reason for Mets fans to watch with hands covering their eyes. Those hands were raised in joy when Franco painted the inside corner on a nasty 3-2 changeup.

Franco and Bonds faced off again two nights later, score tied at two and the go-ahead runner on in the ninth inning of Game 3. And again, David overmatched Goliath, this time swinging. The Mets went on to win that night and the next. Franco posted a third straight scoreless appearance in the NLCS opener but got himself into trouble in Game 2. He was charged with two eighth-inning runs, which briefly tied the Cardinals and Mets at five apiece. New York would get John off the hook in the ninth and eventually into the World Series.

Appropriately for Franco, it was the first Subway Series since 1956. And, equally as fitting, Franco was credited with the only win the Mets would get against the Yankees.

For his postseason career, totaling 15 appearances and 14.1 innings, Franco allowed three earned runs and walked three.

The 2001 season had a different look and, later, a far different feeling. Franco was named the third captain in team history and sported the "C" on the left shoulder of his uniform. Then the events of September 11 understandably held a deep personal effect.

"It felt like somebody just punched you right in the stomach," said Franco, the son of a city sanitation worker, who made extra efforts to assist his community in the wake of the attacks. "And unfortunately, we had some friends who were in the buildings, plus a couple of firemen who I knew . . . it was heart-wrenching for us."

When baseball resumed on September 17 in Pittsburgh, Franco—wearing a New York Fire Department hat—summoned the emotional strength to pitch and wound up with the victory. The Mets, who all wore hats honoring first responders, won seven of their next eight and briefly challenge the division champion Braves down the stretch.

Challenges for Franco were on the horizon—with age and arm problems at the forefront. A December 2001 surgery on his left elbow led to complications and a sequence of setbacks.

Ultimately, an MRI revealed that he needed Tommy John surgery. Unwilling to exit baseball on an injury, a determined Franco made it back in May 2003, appearing in 38 games and notching the last of his 424 saves.

Mets management, figuring the 44-year-old's best days were behind him, put business ahead of allegiance and made no effort to re-sign Franco following a 2004 season in which his ERA ballooned to 5.28 over 46 innings. He made a brief stop in Houston, where he capped his appearance total at 1,119.

Almost every Met, if they hang around long enough, becomes tied to a specific era. Franco is unique in that he stayed through several phases—from the back end of the Davey Johnson tenure through the Bobby Valentine playoff delights and concluding with more dark days of the failed Art Howe experiment.

Franco remains fifth in major-league history in saves, doing so without an overpowering repertoire. Instead, he did it through changing speeds and pinpoint control spiced with those occasional late-inning thrill rides. Never did he fit into the stereotypical reliever mold. But in terms of the city he represented, Franco fit in perfectly.

He took his rightful place in the Mets Hall of Fame in 2012 and serves as both club ambassador and baseball operations advisor—an ideal position for a pitcher who perfectly exemplified the tenacity of New York City.

RELIEF PITCHER—JESSE OROSCO

On December 8, 1978, the Mets relinquished one of the last remaining links to the World Series winners of 1969 and the man who was on the mound when it happened—sending Jerry Koosman to the Minnesota Twins in exchange for a minor leaguer and a player to be named later. Little did the Mets know the player they'd receive on the long end of this trade would be one of the first links to their next championship and the man who'd be on the mound when it took place.

Orosco was at center stage for both climactic moments in 1986. First, the immediate aftermath of a 16-inning epic to finish the Houston Astros in the 1986 NLCS—fanning Kevin Bass with the winning run aboard. Then, in the instant following the World Series triumph—a strikeout of Marty Barrett which led to Orosco flinging his glove skyward and going down to his knees with fists raised before being engulfed by his joyous teammates.

Those moments, separated by 12 days, dominate Mets fans' recollections. But as much as they were the high points of his career, they were mere flashes in Orosco's light year of a baseball life—one which crossed five presidential administrations and four decades.

Before experiencing the mountaintop with the Mets in '86, he had a firsthand look at the franchise during its time in purgatory. In 1979, he benefited from being in an organization akin to a turtle on its back. With New York going nowhere, there was little harm in bringing up a reliever who might otherwise need more minor-league seasoning. Jesse's skills were still raw, making him low-hanging fruit once the team had plans to bring in an arm with far more refined abilities. Within two months, he was back in Triple-A. He would take another step down to Double-A for the entirety of 1980 before climbing back to the majors for good in September 1981.

But Orosco remained far from a finished product heading into the next season. That was certainly the opinion of pitching coach Bill Monbouquette and manager George Bamberger, both of whom felt Jesse nibbled around the strike zone and lacked the requisite aggression. Bamberger taught him tenacity and a better way to throw a slider. Those instructions paid immediate dividends. Orosco pitched far better than a 4-10 record would indicate. Compiling the third-best WAR among Mets, his 2.70 ERA was easily the lowest of those who threw at least 50 innings.

Jesse continued to flourish in 1983 with the best of his 24 seasons and perhaps the finest year by any reliever in Mets history. As a first-time All-Star selectee, he worked 110 innings in 62 games and posted a stellar 1.47 ERA to end up third in the NL Cy Young Award voting. He won a career-best 13 games—including both ends of a doubleheader on July 31. In a time before bullpen roles were clearly defined, Orosco was utilized both for long and short relief. In 1984, he led the Mets with 17 saves as his closing responsibilities increased under the leadership of new manager Davey Johnson. Jesse pitched fewer innings but in more closing situations on a club that improved significantly and had more chances to win. Chosen for the All-Star team for the second straight year, Orosco recorded a career-high 31 saves while maintaining a solid 2.59 ERA.

The emergence of sinkerball-tossing rookie Roger McDowell, who supplanted Doug Sisk as Davey's top right-handed short reliever, ate into Jesse's innings and save chances. Still, Orosco and McDowell developed into the righty-lefty tag team that fortified the Mets bullpen for the next two seasons. While McDowell threw approximately 90 more innings from 1985–86, their save totals were almost identical (Roger had 39, Jesse had 38). Additionally, Orosco's 2.53 ERA over that span was slightly lower than his right-handed cohort.

Jesse Orosco can't hide his emotions after fanning Marty Barrett to end the 1986 World Series.
JERRY COLI/DREAMSTIME

Both played significant roles in the 1986 playoffs, but Jesse became the first to notch three victories in a League Championship Series.

Filed under the heading of "you've got all winter to rest," Orosco appeared in four high-leverage occasions during the

LCS with Houston. In the eighth inning of Game 1, he kept the Astros' slim lead at one by retiring the side. In Game 3, Jesse blanked the Astros for two innings to put a hold on a one-run deficit the Mets would eventually overcome thanks to Lenny Dykstra's walk-off two-run homer. In Game 5, he followed Dwight Gooden's 10 splendid innings with two hitless frames, eventually picking up his second series victory.

It appeared Orosco would get a much-needed rest in Game 6. The visiting Mets trailed 3–0 entering the ninth but would tie it up and eventually grab the lead in the 14th. That's when Orosco returned to the forefront with New York three outs away from a Saturday night date in Queens against the American League champs. Billy Hatcher temporarily spoiled those plans when he sent Orosco's offering deep down the left field line and it careened off the makeshift foul pole screen.

He got through that inning and the next before the Mets posted a three-run 16th. With almost five innings of work logged in the span of 24 hours, Orosco was operating on fumes. His fastball wasn't fooling anyone. The Astros scratched for two in the bottom of the 16th and had the tying and go-ahead runs on base as longball threat Kevin Bass stepped up. Keith Hernandez, in an earlier visit to the mound, implored Orosco to stop throwing his decelerated fastball and stick exclusively to breaking pitches.

"That was my last resort," Orosco said. "They were going with me win or lose on that situation."

Arm tired but mind lucid, he used his breaking ball to strike out Bass on a 3-2 pitch. The Mets had finally extinguished the Astros' competitive fire, exhausted Houston's last-gasp efforts, and exhausted themselves in the process. Catcher Gary Carter and his jubilant teammates joined Orosco near the mound in a mob of euphoria. It wouldn't be the last time.

Orosco's workload was lighter in the World Series, but he'd be placed into high-leverage situations in each of the final two games.

"I had nerves a lot of the time," Orosco said. "But I embraced the pressure and loved it."

Jesse held the Red Sox lead at one in the eighth inning of Game 6 when he got Bill Buckner to fly out with two men on. Shortly after the Mets roared into the lead of Game 7, he inherited another eighth-inning threat. Orosco relieved McDowell—vying for his second six-out save of the series and undoubtably the biggest save of his career—with the tying run on second and the potential go-ahead run on first. He prevented lefty-swinging Rich Gedman from moving the runners over by getting him to line out to Wally Backman at second base. Dave Henderson then struck out on a sweeping curve, and pinch-hitter Don Baylor grounded out to shortstop Rafael Santana.

His task in the ninth was made much easier by Darryl Strawberry's towering homer and by his own unlikely RBI single, which poured extra salt in the Red Sox wound. Ed Romero popped up, Wade Boggs grounded out, and Marty Barrett struck out to send Shea Stadium into delirium and Jesse to the bottom of a Mets mosh pit.

Orosco proved to be New York's most valuable October reliever. He was unscored upon in 5.2 World Series innings, and Game 6 of the NLCS was the lone postseason outing in which he allowed any runs.

The glow of that world championship, and all that went into it, faded fast.

His 1987 ERA rose to 4.44 (some two runs more than last year), and Orosco was often prone to giving up the long ball in key spots. Once regarded as the ace of the bullpen as recently as two years prior, the Mets reconsidered their options—specifically with rookie southpaw Randy Myers.

That contemplation didn't sit well with Orosco, who insisted he be traded rather than demoted. He got his wish. Having supplanted Tug McGraw as the Mets' all-time save leader with 107, Orosco was dealt to the Dodgers that December in a three-team exchange.

From there, he etched another record book entry in what became the longest of baseball voyages. Combining amazing durability with an increased use of left-handed specialists, Jesse wore the threads of nine different teams: first Los Angeles, where he faced (and defeated) his former club in the 1988 play-offs, then Cleveland, then Milwaukee, down to Baltimore, west to St. Louis, back to the Dodgers, down to San Diego, over to the Yankees, and finally to Minnesota—where he established the MLB appearance record at 1,252.

For all the stops made during a career which covered almost a quarter century, it's hard to dispute that his most successful was in Queens. And for all the seasons, teams, games, and pitches, nothing will compare to the exhilaration of October 1986.

2

CATCHERS

STARTING CATCHER—MIKE PIAZZA

Asking a newly acquired superstar to single-handedly lift a franchise into legitimacy is often too much for one player to pull off. Even more so when the swirl of demands arise in New York.

Piazza was the primary conveyor of back-to-back playoff appearances and a National League pennant. The power he displayed in Los Angeles carried over to the Big Apple, as promised. He ensured the Mets were an annual contender, with 101 homers and 313 RBIs through a little more than two seasons.

But September 21, 2001, carried a different significance altogether. Piazza lifted the spirits of a city in despair with his eighth-inning home run in the first professional sports contest held in New York following the devastating terrorist attacks. To Mets fans, baseball fans, and those seeking normalcy in unstable times, he gave a sense of order.

"It was absolute confusion until Mike hit that ball," manager Bobby Valentine said. "And then there was absolute clarity of what we were doing and why we were doing it."

Through the lens of baseball, he was the perfect representative for strength in New York City. How close he came to never playing there.

Some say it's not the journey, it's the destination. But Piazza's road to the Hall of Fame is as unlikely as anyone who's ever been inducted in Cooperstown. A 62nd-round pick from Norristown, Pennsylvania, he was considered nothing more than a courtesy choice by the Dodgers because of the relationship between manager Tommy Lasorda and Mike's father, Vince.

Piazza quickly turned the selection from a favor into a master stroke. From 1993 through 1997, he batted .337 with an average of 33 homers and 105 RBIs—a remarkable showing of well-rounded hitting from a catcher. But he and the Dodgers couldn't come to an agreement on a contract extension. L.A. sent Piazza to the Marlins in a mega-deal. He was embarking on a different journey—as most around baseball knew his destination would be anywhere but Miami, with the Marlins in the midst of a fire sale.

Mike Piazza, arguably the greatest hitting catcher ever, became just the second Hall of Famer to be inducted as a Met.
JERRY COLI/DREAMSTIME

The New York public and media saw an irresistible opportunity for the Mets to sign a potentially transformative figure in the organization—one capable of turning the Mets from plucky overachievers into mighty pennant challengers.

New York had broken a six-year losing season skid with a healthy 88 victories in 1997. The Mets resembled a good team, but one that wasn't going to scare anyone. The fans knew the type of difference maker Piazza could be.

Management waffled at first, but eight days after he transferred to South Beach, Queens got a Piazza delivery—bringing about insatiable buzz, even by New York standards.

"We were doing fine [before him]," Valentine, his manager for five seasons, said. "It was moving along. And when he got here, everything changed. Perception included."

Standing ovations were easy to come by in his May 23 debut—less so in the following weeks. Being anointed as a savior, as Piazza was from the start, had its drawbacks. When he started slowly, with a noticeable lack of power, the public turned on him.

Mike soon settled down and played to the level expected of him. He ended his three-month stint with a .348 average, 23 home runs, and a 1.024 OPS. In batting .378 for September, Piazza was the clear catalyst in New York's fight for a postseason berth.

The Mets withered in the final week—losing their last five games to narrowly miss out on the playoffs. Fans wondered if the dalliance with Piazza, eligible for free agency, was just a May-September romance. The answer came quickly—and with emphasis. The Mets inked him to a record seven-year, $91 million deal that ensured he'd be a New Yorker through his prime. Piazza showed it was money well spent—beginning with a monster 1999.

Piazza set the Mets' single-season RBI record with 124 and came within one of the team's single-year home run mark. As consistent and vital as Piazza was to the cause for five months, he tapered off in the sixth. The 1999 Mets went up and down in late September and October more often than an elevator, and Piazza struggled to carry his club. He hit .200 over the final 28 games (finishing at .303) as occupational hazards wore him down.

New York made the playoffs, but the adrenaline still could not cure what ailed him. Additional carnage absorbed by his body exacted a heavy toll. Piazza was sidelined after playing in the first two games of the NLDS against Arizona. The Mets, though, were not devoid of power from the catching position as Todd Pratt ended the series with a walk-off homer in Game 4. Mike returned to his accustomed starting role for the LCS, but Braves pitching held him in check. He departed the epic Game 5 an inning early after a collision at home plate and was not expected to be a factor even as he limped into the lineup for Game 6 in Atlanta.

The Mets battled back from a 5–0 deficit to get within striking distance in the top of the seventh. Piazza, who'd normally be on the bench or the disabled list if this were a regular-season contest, came up with a runner on and Atlanta clinging to a 7–5 lead. He found the perfect time for his first extra-base hit of the playoffs—an opposite-field homer off John Smoltz. The Mets had dragged themselves off the mat with their battered catcher delivering a devastating punch. Piazza gave way to Pratt later, and New York's playoff odyssey would end in 11 innings.

Through great physical sacrifice, Piazza led the Mets to the doorstep of the Fall Classic. And in 2000, they broke through. As expected, he topped the club in homers for the third straight season, while his .324 batting average tied for the team lead with Edgardo Alfonzo. Piazza also drove in 113 runs. And for 15 consecutive games, spanning from June 14 through July 2, he tallied at least one RBI—two shy of MLB's all-time record.

The streak reached its height on June 30, when he capped one of the best comebacks in team history and turned the tables on the Braves. Down 8–1 to start the eighth inning, a parade of productive at-bats methodically ate at the Atlanta advantage. Five singles, an RBI groundout, and four walks brought New York even. The momentum generated by the rally built and the Shea crowd was ready to explode. Piazza provided the detonation. The first pitch he saw became a tracer down the left field line. As the ball landed fair to complete a 10-run inning, Piazza pumped his fist and fans roared to an ear-popping decibel.

Piazza's superb hitting forgave his perceived shortcomings on defense. The harshest criticism on him was his ability—or lack thereof—to hold opposing baserunners. In fact, he led the league in stolen bases allowed seven times—including in 2000. But he also led the NL in fielding percentage for catchers at .997 and aided a pitching staff that ranked third in ERA.

Those arms delivered again in New York's repeat playoff trip. And a more exciting development was much improved health for Piazza. Even so, he remained quiet through the NLDS win over San Francisco before busting out of a mini-slump with a .412 average in the Mets' five-game NLCS triumph over the Cardinals. The Mets engaged the Yankees in the World Series, but a personal battle took precedence amid the Subway Series hoopla.

When the two teams faced off in the Bronx that July, Yankee aggressor Roger Clemens hit Piazza squarely in the helmet, a pitch Mike claimed was intentional. Their next encounter took place in the first inning of Game 2 and actually exceeded the pre-game hype. Piazza shattered his bat on a foul ball while jogging down the first-base line. Clemens caught and flung a piece in Mike's direction. This run-in with "The Rocket" and, to a lesser extent, his series-ending flyball to Bernie Williams in center field were the enduring moments from his only World Series, one in which he produced two homers and four extra-base hits.

New York was the center of the baseball landscape in October 2000. It would be again 11 months later, in the wake of 9/11. When baseball returned, the Braves came to Shea Stadium. A meeting of NL East rivals in the heat of a pennant race was rendered secondary—replaced by thoughts of lives lost as well as concern and trepidation about whether it was proper and safe to play again. The game served as a brief three-hour opportunity for solace and a temporary distraction from the horror that took place mere miles from the ballpark 10 days before.

The understandably subdued crowd had little reason to cheer for much of the game. Atlanta held a 2–1 advantage into the bottom of the eighth. As Piazza stepped to the plate with one out and a runner on, it was impossible not to conjure up a storybook scenario. He had delivered dramatic late-game home runs many times before, making it central casting for him to write this script.

Almost on cue, Piazza hammered a Steve Karsay pitch. As the ball sailed beyond the fence and into the dark background in deep center field, there was an outpouring of cheers from fans who had been conflicted about when the right time was to exude emotion over a simple baseball game. Now was that time.

The Mets held on to their 3–2 lead. New York City, at least on this night, had something to celebrate.

The Mets late-season bid for the playoffs came up short in 2001, and next year's edition was a categorical disappointment. However, Piazza couldn't be lumped into the pile of under-achievers. Although his average fell below .300 for the first time in his career (.280), he clubbed 33 homers, giving him at least 30 for the ninth time, along with 98 RBIs to take his 10th Silver Slugger Award in as many seasons. All this while weathering trivial and unsubstantiated rumors questioning his sexuality.

As Piazza entered his mid-30s, he began the inevitable decline that comes with working behind the plate. He could only manage 68 games in 2003. And as a method to best pre-serve his bat in 2004, manager Art Howe tried him at first base—an idea Mike initially scoffed at. Piazza eventually conceded, but gave no Keith Hernandez flashbacks during his short tenure.

The Mets were clearly in transition by the middle of the decade. It was even clearer that Piazza, now 35 and not showing the same power or consistent hitting, wouldn't be part of it. He still was an All-Star in his final two years in New York, which gave him six as a Met and 12 overall. On October 2, 2005, in front of nearly 48,000 at Shea, Piazza bid farewell during mul-tiple curtain calls and an eight-minute standing ovation from the appreciative crowd. He finished out his career with single-year stints in San Diego and Oakland.

By comparison, his stats in L.A. over seven seasons (177 homers, 563 RBIs, and a .331 average) stack up more favorably than his numbers in New York over eight seasons (220 home runs, 655 RBIs, .296 average). But when it comes to influence on the fortunes of a baseball team, it's the Mets hands-down. Piazza left no doubt about the organization with which he most associates himself.

"One of the hardest moments of my career was walking off the field at Shea Stadium and saying goodbye," he said in his retirement statement. "My relationship with you made my time in New York the happiest of my career, and for that, I will always be grateful."

Piazza drove in 1,335 runs and posted a .308 career batting average in addition to setting the all-time record for home runs by a catcher with 396—staking his claim as the greatest hitting backstop ever. His quest for the Hall of Fame, however, became a bit murky due to unfounded claims of performance-enhancing drug use. But in 2016, his third year of eligibility, he made it. And justly so, he made it as a Met.

"Looking back into this crowd of blue and orange brings me back to the greatest time of my life," he said during his induction speech. "The thing I miss most is making you cheer."

Reserve Catcher—Gary Carter

If Keith Hernandez was the soul of the 1986 Mets, Gary Carter was the heart. Opposing fans, players, and even his teammates found his wholesome, virtuous persona mawkish, downright nauseating, and phony. Maybe Carter overindulged the media—certainly not the worst characteristic to lay upon a ballplayer. But the media had reason to give him the attention.

Over the course of 12 seasons, Carter became the toast of Montreal. Merging defensive instincts and a power bat, he led the league in nabbing potential base stealers three times and posted six seasons of hitting 20 or more home runs.

Carter, mirroring what Rusty Staub did before him, embraced the French-Canadian culture. Coupled with his expressive love for the game, which earned him the nickname "Kid," his enhanced visibility occasionally rankled those around him. But Carter didn't know any other way.

The All-Star Game served as an ideal showcase for the catcher with the irrepressible smile. He won MVP twice, including in 1984, when he spent two innings catching a young phenom pitcher named Dwight Gooden. It was a sneak preview of what was to come. When Carter joined the Mets before 1985, he shared leadership responsibilities with Hernandez. Both were known for their tenacity and guidance, even if Keith was far less demonstrative.

But like Hernandez, Carter retained a dominant clutch gene. He was a man for the moment—several occurring in the 1986 postseason. Carter provided the winning hit in Game 5 of the NLCS, two home runs in Game 4 of the World Series, and pioneered the indelible rally against the Red Sox three nights later in Game 6.

Carter's overall numbers in New York, during which his aching body would eventually get the better of him, aren't on par with the Hall of Fame–worthy numbers he posted in Montreal. But he had an undisputable impact on vaulting the Mets to the top and doing so with childlike joy and unshakable determination.

A good hitting catcher who can also play solid defense and nurture pitchers is akin to a diamond in the rough. Frank Cashen, the Mets general manager, and just about everyone else who watched knew there was a glaring area of weakness behind the plate. While serviceable, incumbent backstop Mike Fitzgerald provided next to no impact on offense.

When Cashen found out the Expos were in a rebuild, he had come across his rare jewel. Carter—an All-Star, Gold Glover, middle-of-the-order bat, and natural-born leader— checked every box. Even if it took dispatching the popular third baseman Hubie Brooks, it was a deal worth making.

New York went from having a glaring void at catcher to having the best catcher, which created the most anticipation for a Mets season in more than a decade. If the players and the public carried the same sentiment regarding Gary's overzeal-ousness and camera obsession, it would be forsaken if he helped fulfill the promise of championship aspirations.

Carter immediately curried favor. A walk-off homer on Opening Day is a nice way to do that. Carter took former Met Neil Allen deep for a 6–5 win over St. Louis and the Mets began a taut battle with the Cards for NL East supremacy.

While the pitching that Carter oversaw performed to its abilities and the Mets hovered near the top of the NL East, Gary wasn't hitting by his standards. At the All-Star break, he had 11 homers, nine doubles, and 40 RBIs while nagged by an inflamed right knee. Those struggles festered into the second half, which included a month-long homerless stretch.

But as the pennant race heated up, Carter began to sizzle. From the end of August to early October, he recorded 42 hits in the 32-game span (a .331 average), posted an OPS of 1.108, and more than doubled his home run output (15). Included in that homer barrage were three in successive at-bats in San Diego on September 3—the fifth Met to accomplish the long ball trifecta.

It still wasn't enough to overtake the Cards. A tough 4–3 loss at Busch Stadium on October 3, which ended on a Carter flyout, all but wrecked the Mets' playoff hopes despite a 98-win year.

The last big piece to the 1986 championship puzzle, Gary Carter gave the Mets a proven leader who took them to the top.

Despite this, Carter's debut season in New York could be classified as a rousing success: a career-high 32 home runs and 100 RBIs plus fostering the young starting rotation of Gooden, Darling, and Fernandez. The pinnacle of a World Series wasn't far away.

By the next year, New York got what it wanted, and Carter, who had played a dozen years without a ring, got what he came for. The Mets made a mockery of their NL East competition, dispensing with any thoughts of a tight pennant race in 1986. Carter was once again the team's premiere run-producer, setting a Mets' single-season RBI record of 105.

New York was the envy of every other city because players like Carter were regularly taking curtain calls and because of their remarkable depth. Not even a brief thumb injury to Carter in August could do anything to slow down the Mets as they lapped their divisional competition.

Gary returned to the lineup fresh for the postseason, but his bat had yet to show up. Houston ace Mike Scott got in the heads and under the skin of many Mets hitters, Carter foremost among them. Gary suffered a three-strikeout night at the hands of Scott in Game 1 of the NLCS and another 0-fer in Game 4. He voiced accusations toward the eventual Cy Young Award winner of scuffing baseballs to add extra movement to his split-fingered pitch. Met personnel even presented NL president Chub Feeney with alleged Scott-altered balls as evidence.

Carter's frustration lasted deep into Game 5, as the Mets and Astros remained tied at one into the bottom of the 12th. With one out and Wally Backman at second, Keith Hernandez took the open base via an intentional walk. The Astros pitched to Carter—carrying the burden of a 1-for-21 slump. The weight of that drought evaporated when his grounder found its way into center field. Backman beat Billy Hatcher's throw home, and the Mets took a 3-2 series lead back to Houston.

"I kept telling myself, 'I'm going to come through here,'" Carter said postgame. "I knew it was just a matter of time. I'm not an .050 hitter."

New York's trip to Houston lasted only a day. One very long day. Carter worked all of Game 6—from Bob Ojeda's first pitch in the bottom of the first until Jesse Orosco's final pitch in the bottom of the 16th. No amount of innings, time, or drama could subdue Gary's exhilaration when Orosco struck out Kevin Bass to cement New York's 7–6 victory. A first title for Carter was four wins away. But after the first two World Series games at Shea Stadium, the Mets came away winless.

A four-run first inning in Game 3, which featured a Carter double, was the wake-up call New York sorely needed. That 7–1 win furnished momentum for the next night—as Gary slew the Green Monster with a pair of home runs over the 37-foot-high Fenway Park barrier.

Reliance on Carter's bat became imperative as Game 6 reached its crucial stages. In the bottom of the eighth, with the Red Sox up 3–2 and the margin for error small, Gary came up with the bases loaded and none out. On a 3-0 pitch from Calvin Schiraldi, Carter got the green light to swing away and ripped a line drive to left field that turned into a tying sacrifice fly.

In the bottom of the 10th, the margin for error was nonexistent. Hope had all but dissipated. Down 5–3 and down to the last out, there were no contingency plans. Without Carter's single to left, what followed in the at-bats of Kevin Mitchell, Ray Knight, and Mookie Wilson—creating the ultimate moment of Mets ecstasy—would have been a far-fetched fantasy.

The Mets locked up Game 7 with Orosco's strikeout of Marty Barrett, and during the ultimate on-field celebration, Carter's joyfulness—famously captured with his catcher's mask raised in one hand and the glove in the other—was a manifestation of his unabashed enthusiasm.

After 13 years, Carter had the ring that had eluded him several times before. It was the high point in a Hall of Fame career that began its descent the next season as wretched knees seriously impeded his ability. Being "Kid" was true in nickname and demeanor only. He hit .231 from 1987 to 1989 and saw his power numbers regress steadily with each passing year. He did manage to reach 300 career home runs, but only after a lengthy drought leading up to the milestone. Carter was named to the last of his 11 All-Star Games, but a premiere catcher he was not. Baserunners continued to run at will. In 1988, they successfully stole 81 percent of the time.

Carter played most of that year's NLCS, going 6-for-27 with four RBIs—two of which came in the dramatic opener at Dodger Stadium. With two on and two outs in the ninth and the Mets down by a run, Los Angeles aligned its outfielders deep. Jay Howell got two strikes on Carter with breaking balls, then tried another. Gary connected—albeit not sharply. A floater fell just in front of a diving John Shelby in center field. Darryl Strawberry scored easily. Kevin McReynolds followed by barreling into catcher Mike Scioscia before Shelby's throw arrived. The favored Mets won, 3–2, but were stunned in seven games.

Despite initial speculation about his return to New York, Gary stayed with the Mets for 1989. But the troubles he was encountering exacerbated themselves. His heavily bandaged legs left him nearly broken beyond repair. He spent over two months on the disabled list. When he was able to hobble onto the field, Carter was a shell of his former self. Through July 28 and 94 plate appearances, his average sat at .105 and he had managed only one home run. The catching baton had already been passed to Mackey Sasser and Barry Lyons when the home finale arrived, but Davey Johnson insisted Carter get one final appearance before the Shea crowd. Still as much a man for the moment as he was when he debuted, Carter doubled down the left-field line—which led to a standing ovation as he exited the field as a Met for the last time.

It took six tries, and 11 years after retirement, before Hall of Fame voters justly recognized Carter in 2003. He is one of a handful who've caught at least 100 games for 12 consecutive seasons, a feat which can explain why his numbers sharply decreased at the end. Nonetheless, his 324 homers (298 as a catcher), 1,225 RBIs, and superb defense during his prime should've gotten him inducted sooner.

It's hard to comprehend that for all the players on the '86 team who lived so perilously, the first to pass on was one who lived so decently. As the painful reality of brain cancer ultimately took him in February 2012 at age 57, it's impossible to imagine he ever lost that abundance of spirit and the unmistakable smile he became so noted for. Gary Carter didn't know any other way.

RESERVE CATCHER—JERRY GROTE

During his 20-year Hall of Fame career, Tom Seaver was caught by fellow inductees Johnny Bench and Carlton Fisk. But it was Grote, referred to by Seaver as "my catcher," who "The Franchise" felt was the greatest backstop he ever had. This tremendous heap of praise was echoed by other Mets pitchers of that era who benefited from Grote's gruff (but valuable) guidance, even if it took some getting used to.

While nobody will ever consider Bench—the backstop stalwart for the Cincinnati Reds—as anything but the best catcher of the 1970s, Grote mastered the forgotten aspects of a job that necessitates toughness and intellect.

"Catching is a position that doesn't get the publicity that I really feel it should," he once said. "The defensive part of it, especially. If you throw guys out, it's one thing. It might be written up, but it's shortly forgotten. Calling a good ball game—if your pitcher does a real good job, throws the ball just exactly where you call the pitch, it works out great. And more than likely, you're going to get a little ink on it because a pitcher is going to [recognize you]."

Anyone seeking a word from Grote during the game was liable to have their head torn off. Within the confines of the ballpark, he was as comforting as a cactus. Ask retired umpire Bruce Froemming, who claims Grote intentionally let a high fastball get by him while the arbiter was working a game behind the plate. The same went for opponents, the media, and even his teammates.

Grote's intensity to win knew no bounds. But those able to penetrate the exterior shell encountered a much more pleasant side. "Everybody was a no-good son of a bitch to him when he put the uniform on," said Art Shamsky in his book *After the Miracle*. "Once he put on his street clothes, he was the nicest guy."

Shortly after Grote was plucked away from his home state of Texas and the Houston Astros in October 1965, the Mets were desperately seeking catching stability and would withstand any irritability. From 1966 to 1968, Grote threw out 44 percent of would-be base stealers and averaged more than 59 assists and more than 626 putouts per year. However, his cantankerous nature sometimes reared its ugly head. Without any backup catchers available, he got himself tossed from a July 1967 game and was subsequently fined by manager Wes Westrum.

Gil Hodges took over for Westrum in 1968 and understood the importance of strength up the middle. Grote's firm counseling, when marshalled properly, could help accelerate the progress of a promising pitching staff.

"I hesitate to imagine where the New York Mets would have been the last few years without Jerry," Hodges told *Sports Illustrated* in 1971. "He is invaluable to us. He is intent and intense and he fights to get everything he can."

Neither Tom Seaver in his second season nor Jerry Koosman in his first were threatened by Grote's irascibility. And it didn't take long for mutual respect to develop.

Strong cajoling from Grote, Hodges, and pitching coach Rube Walker helped Seaver and Koosman combine for 35 victories and collectively post an ERA slightly above 2.00. Both made the All-Star Game along with Grote, who threw out 30 of 69 potential base stealers and allowed only one passed ball in 1,005 innings. Additionally, he led the team in on-base percentage at .357 and was second best in batting average at .282.

It was clear that the Mets' strength was in their battery. That strength could help take them beyond where they'd ever been. Grote had a premonition before 1969, even if he didn't necessarily make a declaration. Many others were optimistic, but Grote believed his fellow Mets were setting their sights too low. He was bold enough, and prescient also, to make that claim in spring training.

"When you play together a few years, you get to know each other and things improve. . . . There's a different feeling on the team this year," he said. "There's more togetherness. There's more pride. We're a close-knit team."

Defying pre-season predictions and affirming Grote's confidence, the Mets hovered above the .500 mark heading into the summer before closing in on the first-place Chicago Cubs in late August.

It was probably around this time that those teammates started to feel Grote was actually on to something. But he certainly wasn't all talk. Part of the credit for the overall success of a pitching staff laden with inexperience (10 of the 15 had been tenured for two years or fewer) must be attributed to his command behind the plate. This was especially evident during the season's final months. From August 1 onward, Met arms posted a 2.32 ERA and 17 shutouts as New York went 45-18. Grote started 39 games during that stretch, batting .307 while manufacturing 15 percent of the scoring. He produced 12 multi-hit performances, including a 2-for-4 effort on the same night Gary Gentry tossed a four-hit blanking of the St. Louis Cardinals to secure the NL East crown.

His six home runs and 40 RBIs were career highs. Defensively, he had a .991 fielding percentage and his caught stealing rate of 56.3 percent ranked second among NL catchers.

Grote played 113 games, splitting time with backups J. C. Martin and Duffy Dyer in Hodges's platoon system. But there was no replacing him in the postseason. Grote called every pitch, including the World Series, during which Mets hurlers held the potent Orioles to a collective .146 batting average.

Grote's hunch crystallized into something beyond anyone's imagination. But reality would set in following the World Series

Toughness is a prerequisite for catchers. Jerry Grote had more than most.
NATIONAL BASEBALL HALL OF FAME

triumph. As is commonplace for most backstops, his tenacity could only carry him so far. The physical toll of two seasons of catching 126 and 125 contests, respectively, began to show as Grote could throw out only 33 percent of base stealers between 1970 and 1971.

His capacity to stay behind the plate began to suffer further. Grote missed almost two-thirds of the '72 schedule and nearly half of the next year. Fortunately, he was relatively healthy for the stretch run in '73 to aid the Mets as they made a sudden rise from last place to first. Jerry returned from a forearm fracture in July and batted .300 after August 3, hitting safely in six of the final eight games.

Just like '69, Grote didn't miss a moment behind the plate in the 1973 postseason. But the heavy workload worked to his detriment. Having labored through 22 innings in Games 2 and 3 of the World Series against Oakland, with a cross-country trip in between, Grote's reflexes were severely tested. That frailty came into effect in the 11th inning of the third game, when a passed ball paved the way for the go-ahead run in a series the A's would win in seven.

Grote absorbed more hard knocks in 1974. The nicks and bruises impeded his ability to throw runners out (down to 35 percent) or stay on the field. He still managed to make his second All-Star Game, but a foul ball off his hand forced him to miss the final month in a lost season for the fifth-place Mets.

The Mets, aware of his gradual deterioration, sought fresh catching help ahead of 1975, but Grote proved that whomever was behind him would have to wait. Back problems and a strained shoulder couldn't stop Grote from having his most productive year offensively. He compiled a .295 batting average on top of a league-leading .995 fielding average and six pickoffs while playing 111 games at backstop—his most since 1971.

The injuries that did little to prevent him from a great '75 got ahold of him in '76. Catching 95 games, Grote fielded at a .993 clip and hit .272. But chronic back issues persisted and limited him to just four games in the final month of the season. This prompted the Mets to take a more serious look at a younger option behind the plate, namely John Stearns—nine years Grote's junior and a more dependable batter. Grote could see his grasp on the starting catching role slipping away and contemplated retirement. Instead, he opted to mentor the 25-year-old Stearns in spring training of 1977.

The limitations the Mets had at other positions allowed Grote to be used at third base in addition to backing up Stearns, who went on to his first All-Star Game. But no more than a month-and-a-half later, and nearly two months after the Mets notoriously traded away his legendary battery mate Seaver, Grote went farther west and joined the Dodgers in a deal for two minor leaguers.

From the perspective of Mets history, the subsequent periods of Gary Carter and Mike Piazza obscure Grote's tremendous impact on this franchise during his 12 seasons. A player's value is dictated by the organization's focus and formula for success. On a pitching-centric team from the late 1960s through the mid-1970s, he was in the right place at the right time. Grote's best assets behind the plate were hard to evaluate. A better method of judgment is to hear the opinions of those qualified to speak about it.

"If Jerry Grote were a Cincinnati Red," said Johnny Bench, "I would have been a third baseman."

3

FIRST BASEMEN

Starting First Baseman—Keith Hernandez

He knew what everyone else did in 1983: Shea Stadium was a major-league abyss. When Hernandez got word he'd be leaving the reigning champion St. Louis Cardinals for a moribund franchise mired in the cellar, the drastic change caused Hernandez to evaluate his future.

"The Mets deserved and received no respect," said Hernandez, winner of a batting title and NL co-MVP in 1979. "And here I was, coming over from the world champions to a team with four last-place finishes in six years, and the other two next-to-last. Banished. Shipped to the Siberia of baseball."

In GM Frank Cashen's efforts to restore respectability, he had cultivated promising prospects that had reached—or were approaching—the big-league level. But no amount of veteran leadership would come from the farm system. At the 1983 trade deadline—ironically, six years to the evening from when the franchise broke with relevancy by shipping away Tom Seaver—Cashen pulled a coup that put the Mets rebuild on the accelerator.

Hernandez and St. Louis manager Whitey Herzog, a former Mets director of player development, were at odds—primarily due to Herzog's perception of Keith's lackadaisical play and alleged cocaine use.

Like a present from a heaven-sent carrier pigeon, the Cardinals first baseman was plopped in New York's lap—and all the Mets had to give up was a declining relief pitcher and another arm which would make seven more big-league starts and win once. In short, this was grand larceny.

The Mets were elated to be getting a player of Hernandez's caliber. Unfortunately, the feeling wasn't initially mutual. As Keith headed into free agency later that year, staying in New York was far from a certainty. He batted .306 over 95 games, maintained his streak of NL Gold Glove Awards, and quickly cemented himself as a team leader. But another last-place finish did little to allay Hernandez's skepticism.

Cashen's persuasion strategy centered on the promise in the minors, while Rusty Staub chimed in and spoke from experience about the benefits of playing and living in the Big Apple.

Keith was sold. The greatest trade in Mets history was about to reap its benefits.

"Whitey thought he was going to bury my ass in New York when he traded me here," Hernandez said. "He had no idea what the minor-league system was like. He thought he was going to stick me here to suffer for two years. Didn't happen. There was such a wealth of talent."

That talent needed guidance to grow into its potential and Keith was the perfect pilot. He possessed a sheer force of personality and keen awareness of his surroundings that established confidence in his teammates, often conferencing with pitchers on the mound or lending advice to hitters in the dugout. From this confidence eventually came respect from opponents and a winning attitude that hadn't been felt in Queens for almost a decade.

Almost nothing could get by Keith Hernandez—not a grounder, a bunt, or many good pitches. In seven seasons, Keith won six Gold Gloves and hit over .300 three times.
JERRY COLI/DREAMSTIME

During his first five full seasons, Hernandez participated in more victories and gained more MVP support than any other player in the National League. Said former Mets broadcaster

Tim McCarver: "I've never seen a man 'in the game' as much as Keith Hernandez."

He was a meticulous hitter who dissected at-bats the way he pored over a *New York Times* crossword puzzle in the clubhouse. His diligence didn't go without reward. Keith batted over .300 three times, had the highest batting average among Mets hitters with at least 3,000 at-bats, and drove in at least 83 runs each year from 1984 to 1987.

But what distinguished him as the most unique of first basemen was the way he expanded the capabilities of a position rarely noted for exemplary defense. Keith charged toward the plate on potential bunts, which directly affected the way opposing teams sacrificed. He displayed range rarely seen before and turned infielder's bad throws into outs. Hernandez won the Gold Glove in each of his first six seasons in New York, extending his streak to a record 11.

His intangibles could also be measured—specifically in how the Mets improved in 1984. The swift organizational attitude adjustment Keith fostered took effect that year. As runner-up for NL MVP, he batted .311, smacked 15 homers, 31 doubles, and drove in 94, often using his cerebral knowledge of the strike zone to generate a key hit at will. The Mets kept pace with the division-winning Cubs into September. Ultimately, they ended with 90 victories—22 more than in 1983.

Before Hernandez, the Mets thought they could win. Now, they knew they would.

Keith couldn't do it alone, though. His guidance wouldn't mean much if more talented pieces weren't in place. Enter Gary Carter, similar in leadership quality, yet vastly different in outward emotion. With the two veterans at the forefront, New York improved to 98 wins and was entrenched in an even tighter pennant race in 1985. But it was by no means a joyride for Hernandez.

While he posted stats comparable to 1984—leading the team in runs, walks, hits, doubles, and batting average—and became one of a handful of Mets to hit for the cycle, doing so in a zany 19-inning contest that began on the night of Independence Day, the comfort Keith felt on the field was negated by squirm-inducing personal troubles.

In September, the Pittsburgh Drug Trials called on Hernandez to testify. There, he admitted to having previously used cocaine. By cooperating, Hernandez was granted immunity from prosecution. He accepted a commuted sentence to donate a portion of his salary to drug-related causes and perform community service.

Mere days after returning to action following the testimony, Keith delivered a ninth-inning single to beat the Cardinals and briefly put the Mets in sole possession of first place—a lead they wouldn't hold, but would serve as motivation for 1986.

With off-field distractions subsiding, Hernandez played his part in the most dominant Mets season ever. Keith didn't have a career year in '86, but like Strawberry, Gooden, and Carter, he didn't need to. Hernandez topped the Mets in walks for the fourth straight year, and his 94 free passes led the league. He batted .310 and produced the best on-base percentage since his co-MVP campaign of 1979. The regular season was simply a prelude to a highly anticipated postseason, which began with an NLCS meeting with Houston. As was the case with just about every other Met, Keith couldn't solve the quandary presented by Astros ace Mike Scott. New York, in fact, had difficulty against the entire Houston rotation—scoring just 11 runs through five games yet still holding a 3-2 series edge. In order to avoid Scott again, the Mets needed to end it in six. This was the closest thing to a must-win scenario without actually facing elimination.

Even the smartest of players seek out others for insight regardless of whether they're in the ballpark or not. Bob Knepper was the pitcher causing the Mets angst this time—as he preserved a 3–0 lead through eight innings. Keith started the afternoon 0-for-3 when he went into the clubhouse to phone his brother Gary, who Keith regularly counted on for help, to ask if his swing was alright. Gary said he was too tentative.

Sound advice. With one runner on and one run in, Hernandez ripped at Knepper's offering and drove it into the right-center field gap. Mookie Wilson scored to bring the Mets closer. New York soon made up the rest of the difference, forced extras, took the lead in the top of the 14th, lost the lead in the bottom of the 14th, took it back with three runs in the top half of the 16th, and held on for dear life to advance to the World Series.

That epic was over. Another was on-deck.

The Mets created more dramatic situations for themselves, beginning with a pair of home losses. The Red Sox broke open Game 2 on an uncharacteristic Hernandez throwing error, but the Mets woke up at Fenway Park. Keith had two of New York's 13 Game 3 hits but was just two for his next 11. The last of those 11 at-bats was a flyball to dead center field in the bottom of the 10th inning of Game 6, caught near the warning track by Dave Henderson.

A distraught Hernandez, understandably assuming the season was almost over, stormed through the dugout. Just like in Game 6 of the NLCS, he proceeded to the clubhouse. This time not for advice but for solace, drowning his sorrows with a Budweiser while perched in manager Davey Johnson's office.

As Gary Carter and Kevin Mitchell staved off defeat with singles, Keith dared not mess with superstition.

"That chair has hits in it," he recalled. "And I stayed right there."

The Mets stayed alive for another day. Actually, two. A Sunday rainout pushed Game 7 to Monday, when Keith became the focal point in another comeback.

Bruce Hurst limited the Mets to one hit through five shutout innings before New York came to life in the sixth with singles from Lee Mazzilli and Mookie Wilson and a Tim Teufel walk. Keith strode to the plate down by three. He didn't have to reach far into his memory to recall an eerily similar situation.

"I remember that well," Hernandez said in the postgame celebration, remarking on his two-run bases-loaded single in the sixth inning of the deciding game of the 1982 World Series, helping his Cardinals prevail over the Brewers. Just like he did four years earlier, Keith delivered. A hit to left-center sent home Mazzilli and Wilson and sent Shea into a frenzy.

"I had swung the bat great all series," Keith said. "I told [my brother] this morning 'If I get up with men on base tonight, I'm going to be the man.'"

The Mets went on to score another in that inning, three more in the seventh, and two in the eighth to put the Red Sox away.

The only honors Keith would receive in 1987 would be of the personal variety—named the first Mets captain, claiming another Gold Glove, and selected to his fifth All-Star Game (managed by Davey Johnson). Diverting slightly from his contact-centric approach, Hernandez was a bit more feast or famine. He set a career high in home runs (18) while also exceeding 100 strikeouts for the first time and posting his lowest batting average since he was 24 years old.

Entering the 1988 season, Keith was now 34—senior citizen territory for a major leaguer. With age making him more susceptible to injury, Keith was no longer immune from the disabled list. He would win the last of his 11 Gold Gloves, but he was no longer batting around .300 and wasn't getting on base as frequently. Yet his presence on the field and the importance of him being at first base remained just as vital. With Hernandez missing from the lineup because of a hamstring pull, the Mets sputtered at 35-32. When he was active, the Mets were 65-30. That included a stretch in which New York won 29 of its last 39 to pull away from its NL East competition.

It was his last chance to reach another World Series, and it would end in disappointment. In a seven-game loss to Los Angeles, Keith went 7-for-26, the same showing he had against Houston in the '86 NLCS, but few were hits of significance.

The once-durable first baseman was fragile again in 1989. A collision with Dodger second baseman Dave Anderson fractured his kneecap and laid Keith down for two months. This injury proved too severe and the Mets were too far behind for Hernandez's return to have the effect it did in '88. It became clear New York was nothing more than a second-place team, just as it was equally apparent management wouldn't renew Keith's contract. Hernandez wrapped up his Mets playing days with a modest .233 average and eventually fell off the major-league radar with a brief stay in Cleveland. But he wouldn't be out of the limelight for long.

Following retirement in 1990, Hernandez parlayed his intuitive baseball knowledge and general acerbic wit into a successful broadcasting career that has enhanced his popularity—if his legendary *Seinfeld* cameo didn't do it already. Similar to the effect he had in converting the Mets into respected winners,

Keith understands the effect his career in New York had in turning him into something of a pop culture icon.

"A younger generation knows me," he said. "Baseball reaches a certain segment of society; *Seinfeld* reached the entire nation. It gave me a second life. I think it made everything possible that's going on today; it was a great springboard for me."

RESERVE FIRST BASEMAN—JOHN OLERUD

Reliable, consistent, understated—all traits which perfectly describe Olerud. There's irony in the fact that he had an unmistakable appearance—a flapless helmet worn in the field. It had nothing to do with making a fashion statement. It had everything to do with upholding a promise to his parents that he'd protect his head following a 1989 brain aneurysm.

Three seasons usually isn't enough to create a lasting impact with a franchise. But Olerud had a knack for efficiency. His steady production at the plate and trustworthiness on defense made him an exception to the rule.

"What I remember most about Olerud is that he was exactly what you would expect him to be if all your knowledge of him came simply from watching him play," broadcaster Howie Rose wrote in his 2013 book. "There's an intellect to the way he hit. There's a smoothness to the way he defended. There's an almost inconspicuousness about his persona."

Olerud didn't have the time to accrue the totals that compare with other Mets hitting greats, but he had no trouble getting his name in the franchise record book. At .315, he's still the team's all-time leading hitter. And at .354 in 1998, he remains the keeper of the highest single-season batting average. His sharp eyes and awareness of the strike zone also allowed him to establish the single-season high for on-base percentage at .447

(20 points better than his next closest competitor—himself, a year later). For his Mets tenure, Olerud's on-base mark of .425 has yet to be equaled. John's patience was rewarded further in 1999, when he waited out 125 walks, the most any Met has ever accumulated in one year. Olerud also remains first in career OPS (.926) and second to Darryl Strawberry in adjusted OPS+ (142).

During the power-saturated era of the late 1990s, Olerud showed that the execution of a bases on balls or a single can be invaluable to a club's well-being. His home run average of 21 over his Mets career is modest in relation to his contemporaries. But in a lineup that included heavy hitters like Mike Piazza, Robin Ventura, and Edgardo Alfonzo, his plate discipline gave the Mets more chances to score.

Olerud was also adept at preventing runs. Although he never added to his Gold Glove collection in New York, his fielding percentage rates up there with Keith Hernandez in his heyday.

The Mets acquired Olerud through a trade with the Toronto Blue Jays before the 1997 season, but they could have had him 11 years before that. As a high school player, they selected him in the 27th round of the 1986 amateur draft. John chose not to sign and went on to a legendary collegiate career at Washington State. He made his way back into the Mets organization after eight productive seasons, two World Series titles, three Gold Gloves, and a batting crown. Olerud's disposition left no thought he'd be anything but the same player in New York once he changed teams and leagues. That belief was upheld.

He quickly found the National League to his liking. Better utilizing his fluid swing so that he could spray balls to all fields, Olerud batted 20 points higher than his final year in Toronto.

John Olerud was utterly dependable in the field and at bat. He remains the career and single-season leader in batting average and on-base percentage.
MARK DUNCAN/AP/SHUTTERSTOCK

His 102 RBIs, 22 homers, and 34 doubles were the most since his stellar 1993 season. And on September 11, he became the seventh Met to hit for the cycle.

Olerud's chances to hone those impressive numbers were helped greatly in May 1998. The trade for Mike Piazza boosted the confidence of all Mets, but the power-hitting catcher's insertion into the cleanup spot behind Olerud gave him an opportunity to see quality pitches more frequently. Less than two months after Piazza's arrival, Olerud went on a 23-game hitting streak. In September, he reached base 15 consecutive times, tying Barry Bonds's National League record and coming one successful at-bat short of Ted Williams's all-time mark. After the streak, he proceeded to go 24-for-42 to finish out the season.

Although Piazza's presence overshadowed the rest of the lineup, Olerud's importance to the Mets that year cannot be overstated. He fortified his record .354 batting average and .447 on-base mark with 96 walks to 73 strikeouts. His 307 total bases were assembled through 22 homers, 197 hits, and 36 doubles. Olerud also drove in 93 runs, giving him the team lead for the second consecutive year and he ranked third in the league in wRC+ at 167.

His remarkable consistency found new heights in 1999, when he reached base in 43 straight games. But just as the Mets were struggling to hold on to a playoff berth, Olerud went into—by his standards—a rare slump. His batting average dipped below .300 for the first time since April 9, and he ended at .298. He still accumulated 96 RBIs and was fourth in the NL with 125 walks.

After the Mets managed to sneak into the playoffs, Olerud didn't allow an atypical rough patch to spiral into a bigger one. Against Randy Johnson and his Arizona Diamondbacks, there was no time to cower. Johnson's heat from the first-base side of the pitching rubber was liable to make even the most confident left-handed hitters quake in their cleats. Lefties had hit .103 without a home run against Johnson that year, suffering 35 strikeouts in 87 at-bats.

But in the third inning of the opening game of the NLDS in Phoenix, Johnson left a pitch in the heart of the zone. Olerud turned on it, sending it 10 rows deep into the right-field stands in a contest the Mets would eventually take, 8–4.

That homer kicked Olerud back into gear. He torched Arizona pitching to the tune of a .438 average on his way to a .349 mark for the entire postseason. He also provided two more home runs in each of the Mets' NLCS victories over Atlanta.

As New York looked to avoid a Braves sweep and snap a 15-inning scoreless drought, Olerud took it upon himself to provide all the offense the Mets would need. He went deep with a bases-empty homer in the sixth off John Smoltz. Then, with the Mets trailing 2–1 and four outs from elimination, he faced John Rocker. About the only thing these two had in common was that they both threw left-handed. Rocker, the loud-mouth reliever who unabashedly ripped New Yorkers in general and Mets fans specifically, had dealt Olerud a frustrating hand—0-for-9 with five strikeouts.

But on the fifth pitch, after a double steal put two runners in scoring position, Olerud smacked a grounder up the middle. It glanced off the glove of shortstop Ozzie Guillen and went into center field. As Roger Cedeño and Melvin Mora sped home, Shea Stadium jolted back to life.

Olerud once more carried the New York offense for the better part of Game 5. He lifted a towering two-run shot to right-center field off Greg Maddux to put the Mets on the board early. It would be the only runs they would produce until the bottom of the 15th, when New York erased Atlanta's slim one-run lead with a bases-loaded walk and then won it on the hitting heroics of Robin Ventura.

The Mets were able to learn from their series defeat to the Braves and get past the NLCS and into the World Series in 2000—only it would be without Olerud manning first base. The lure of remaining with a contender couldn't overcome the pull of being home. In December '99, after much contemplation, John chose to join the Seattle Mariners.

"I think if it was any team other than the Mets, it would have been a real easy decision," Olerud said.

He departed the way he performed: quiet and unassuming. That's what makes him among the most underrated Mets. When ranking the franchise players with the greatest total WAR, an accrued statistical measure, Olerud is 21st. That's higher than Ron Darling and just behind Cleon Jones, both of whom had much lengthier careers in New York. Olerud played with the Mets long enough to make a great impression but not so long that he overstayed his welcome.

4

SECOND BASEMEN

STARTING SECOND BASEMAN—EDGARDO ALFONZO

Nolan Ryan, Lenny Dykstra, and Daniel Murphy rank as some of the Mets' finest draft discoveries. Alfonzo doesn't crack this list only because he was never drafted. In what would become a narrative for much of his New York career, Alfonzo went overlooked when it came time to select amateurs in 1991.

The Mets took a flyer on the man they'd affectionately refer to as "Fonzie," signing him as an undrafted free agent. It's impossible to imagine the organization knew that it was getting the seventh-most valuable player in terms of WAR when the deal was struck. If so, the Mets would have nabbed him earlier.

When he began steadily progressing up the minor-league system, they knew for sure. Alfonzo officially climbed to the major-league summit with a promotion to the Mets at the advent of the 1995 season. Before long, he was a regular entrant in manager Dallas Green's starting lineup. But where he played stayed in question.

For his first two years, he split time at second base, third base, and shortstop. In 1997 and 1998, to accommodate Carlos Baerga, Alfonzo played all but 16 games at third. To make room for hot corner Gold Glover Robin Ventura, he shuffled over to second base, where he played three straight seasons before shifting once more to third during his final Mets season in 2002. The positional zigzagging contradicted both his consistent output and steady demeanor.

Fonzie batted better than .300 on four occasions, finishing his time in New York with a .292 mark—the sixth-best by any Met with at least 1,000 at-bats. Four times he led the club in runs scored. Twice he was the team leader in on-base percentage, including an outstanding .425 mark in 2000. For his career, he was .367. His total of 1,136 hits still ranks fifth-highest in franchise history. And three times he led the Mets in hits, topping out at 191 in 1999, which was clearly becoming Alfonzo's breakout season.

He had been two years removed from becoming a permanent fixture on new manager Bobby Valentine's lineup card, leading the club with 163 hits, a .315 batting average, and only trailing John Olerud in on-base percentage at .391. Alfonzo not only retained the qualities that came to fruition in '97, he expanded on them with a power surge that strengthened the Mets batting order into one of the National League's most potent. That still didn't quite turn Alfonzo into a superstar even if his performance warranted it.

Alfonzo proved that it was possible to be overlooked in New York City. The greatest extent of his national recognition, aside from the Mets being a constant presence on television, came when *Sports Illustrated* featured him, Olerud, Robin Ventura, and Rey Ordoñez on a September '99 cover, suggesting the group was the best infield ever.

It was hard to argue against it. While the quartet's 33 errors were the second fewest since 1900, Fonzie ensured his spot as an elite second baseman by leading the NL in fielding percentage (with only five errors) and winding up third in assists and double plays.

Edgardo Alfonzo was an under-the-radar superstar in a city that usually overvalues talent. From 1997 to 2000, he batted .305, averaging 34 doubles and 88 RBIs.
JERRY COLI/DREAMSTIME

Even if he had somehow escaped the publicity, Alfonzo found a way to stand alone in the Mets record book. August 30, 1999, was not only the most brilliant night of his major-league career, but the greatest single-game hitting performance in team history. They called Houston's Astrodome a pitcher's park. Alfonzo, though, chose its spacious dimensions to bust out of a rare 3-for-30 slump.

By the time the dust cleared on Alfonzo's offensive explosion, he had set three club records and tied another. He became the first Met ever to collect six hits and the seventh to blast three homers. His 16 total bases put Fonzie in even more esteemed company. At the time, only 17 others in major-league annals had reached that mark in a nine-inning contest since the turn of the 20th century.

Even in the wake of a one-man show that would make the modest a bit self-congratulatory, Alfonzo maintained his unassuming nature when asked about his favorite part of the evening. "The last out, because we won the game," acknowledging the 17–1 obliteration of the Astros. "I don't think it's going to be good if you have the numbers and you lose the game."

By the conclusion of the 1999 regular season, the numbers he put up a dazzling picture of his well-rounded hitting ability.

Alfonzo combined a .304 average and an on-base percentage of .385 with 27 homers, which were 10 more than the previous high he had established the year before. The 108 RBIs were 30 more than the previous season. Additionally, he displayed an absence of nerves in pressure spots and was a player who could be counted on as much as Mike Piazza. But for Alfonzo to show poise in a pressurized situation like the playoffs, the Mets first had to make the playoffs—a task easier said than done.

It should've happened in 1998, when Alfonzo showed more power (with 17 homers) and knocked in more runs and doubles than ever before. However, New York crumbled down the stretch, dropping its last five to fall one short of a wild card, despite Fonzie going 6-for-14 in the concluding series against Atlanta (and 3-for-5 in the finale).

The Mets barely avoided a similar collapse in '99, saved by Al Leiter on the mound and Alfonzo at the plate in a one-game wild card showdown against Cincinnati.

Leiter's two-hit shutout justifiably garnered headlines. But in this do-or-die affair that determined a spot in the National League Division Series, Alfonzo's two-run first-inning bomb to straightaway center field eased any tension Leiter might have had. The early gut punch, plus Leiter's pitching, kept the Reds from mounting any threat.

It was rare for Alfonzo to let a big October moment pass him by. Fonzie received and seized another opportunity the very next night as the Mets made their first postseason appearance since 1988 against an Arizona Diamondbacks team participating in the playoffs after just two years of existence.

Alfonzo delivered another top-of-the-first-inning homer, this time off eventual Cy Young winner Randy Johnson. But the Mets would need him to do a bit more if they wanted to start the NLDS with a victory. The D-Backs rallied from a 4–1 deficit to tie it. Johnson was still on the mound in the ninth before the Mets wore him down with a pair of singles and a walk. Arizona manager Buck Showalter felt a right-hander, Bobby Chouinard, could solve Alfonzo in a bases-loaded face-off.

Alfonzo promptly made Showalter pay. The deposit: a grand slam around the left-field foul pole—the first such occurrence in Mets playoff history and the difference in an 8–4 win.

His output for the remainder of the postseason was far more understated. Fonzie clubbed another homer against Arizona in Game 4, opening the scoring in a contest remembered for how it ended: the 10th-inning walk-off blast by Todd Pratt. He began the NLCS against Atlanta with two multi-hit games. Then, with the Mets on the brink of elimination in an epic Game 5 at Shea, he offered a sacrifice bunt that moved runners into scoring position and reinforced New York's winning rally. If Alfonzo was still among the most underrated in baseball entering 2000, he wouldn't be after.

The departure of Olerud to Seattle shifted Fonzie from the number-two man in the batting order to number three. Now as Mike Piazza's lead-in, Alfonzo saw a host of quality pitches. A .324 average with 25 homers and 94 RBIs shows he seldom put any of them to waste. Alfonzo was second to Piazza in home runs, runs batted in, and slugging percentage. But he matched Mike in batting, had a far better on-base mark, 20 more hits (176), and 14 more doubles (40).

As he and the Mets returned to postseason play, Alfonzo somehow became even more consistent at the plate. He hit safely during the first 11 games of the 2000 playoffs, extending his overall postseason streak to 13 dating back to '99.

"When we get in a situation where we need a hit," said teammate Darryl Hamilton, "everybody on this team wants Fonzie at the plate."

That's what the Mets got in Game 3 of the NLDS, as Alfonzo keyed a comeback on the San Francisco Giants. A two-out double to left field in the bottom of the eighth helped prolong the contest into extra innings—won on Benny Agbayani's decisive homer in the 13th.

Alfonzo would go on to drive in five runs in the series against San Francisco, including two in the clinching Game 4. Over the first 10 games of this postseason—which included the NLDS, the NLCS with St. Louis, and the World Series versus the Yankees—Alfonzo tallied an RBI in eight of them.

He would've preferred a different time to fall into a slump, but that was the unfortunate condition of his only Fall Classic appearance. Alfonzo could manage just three hits, none for extra bases, in a five-game defeat to the Mets' crosstown rivals.

Just as Alfonzo was receiving the recognition he had long deserved, his body slowly began to give out. It became the underlying pattern for his final two seasons in Queens. Thus, his production tailed off. He hit just .243, with 17 homers and 49 RBIs for 2001. An injured back landed him on the disabled list from mid-June to early July but troubled him for the remainder of the schedule.

Despite the down year, the Mets offered Alfonzo a three-year contract extension worth $18 million in the spring of 2002, which he turned down. He was able to lift his average more to his caliber at .308, but homer and RBI totals (16 and 56, respectively) continued to exemplify his decline. The cause, again, was injuries. His left hand bothered him for a significant portion of the first half due to an ill-fated dive. He logged more time on the disabled list with a strained oblique muscle in August. The 2002 season also led to a return to third base, since the Mets had traded Robin Ventura in the offseason and acquired aging future Hall of Famer Roberto Alomar to play second.

Although his heart (and home) was in New York, the better contract offer (four years and $26 million) was in San Francisco.

His surroundings would change for 2003 but not the physical hurdles.

Upon his departure to the Bay Area, Alfonzo showed his gratitude and class when he purchased $1,500 worth of advertising space atop city taxi cabs with messages that read: "FONZIE LOVES NEW YORK" and "EDGARDO THANKS YOU." Because of his composure in clutch situations, fan friendliness, and sheer dependability, that feeling is very much reciprocated.

RESERVE SECOND BASEMAN—DANIEL MURPHY

Seven homers in a 13-day postseason stretch. Six in consecutive games. It still seems inconceivable, especially when you take note of the modest power threat who did it.

Over 903 games as a Met, Murphy totaled 62 home runs—an average of 12 per season. He equaled that full standard in 2009 ... and actually led the team. But Murphy was most efficient with hits that stayed inside the park. In that respect, he averaged 174 (per 162 games) over his seven years. He surpassed the 30-double level five times, compiled 40 in 2012, and completed his New York career with 228—third-most in Mets history behind David Wright and José Reyes.

But while his hitting was consistent, his running and defense were anything but. Whether in the field or on the base paths, the possibilities were endless and unpredictable. Making a dazzling play, messing up a routine grounder, taking the extra base on a hit, bypassing a stop sign from the third-base coach and getting thrown out. The scale for measuring Murphy's decision-making ranged from brilliant to perplexing.

Those flaws, though, were forgiven and forgotten in October 2015, when Murph masqueraded as a combination of Babe Ruth and Reggie Jackson with a home run binge for the ages.

His first victim was Clayton Kershaw, who he took deep in the fourth inning of the NLDS opener at Dodger Stadium. He waited a few days before duplicating the feat at Citi Field. A Mets loss forced a deciding contest back in Los Angeles, when Murphy delivered the pivotal blow in Game 5. A sixth-inning drive down the left field line off Zack Greinke broke a 2–2 tie and was the difference in New York advancing to the NLCS against the Cubs. Murphy's power display was only getting started.

He wasted little time in Game 1, homering in the first inning of a 4–2 Mets win. The next night he homered in the first inning of a 4–1 New York victory. At Wrigley Field in Game 3, Murphy's third-inning homer vaulted the Mets into a lead they wouldn't relinquish. And in the late stages of Game 4, with the Mets' sweep of the Cubs imminent, he belted a two-run blast over the ivy-covered center-field wall. That capped off a nine-game stretch in which Murphy batted .421 with 16 hits to complement the unprecedented longball barrage. In the NLCS alone, he hit an astonishing .529. The seven postseason homers were one short of the all-time record. But by homering in six straight games, he stood alone.

Nobody could wrap their head around Murphy's out-of-body experience. Not even Murphy.

"I can't explain it," he said. "It's just such a blessing to be able to contribute to what we've been able to do. . . . I'm excited to be able to do something to help us win ball games, but I can't explain it."

Far less stunning than the performance was the formality of naming him LCS MVP. But the inevitable recession occurred in the World Series. In truth, it was a slump well below even Murphy's ordinary standards. He hit just .150 and struck out

In October 2015, Daniel Murphy had a postseason home-run exhibition like no other.
JERRY COLI/DREAMSTIME

seven times in the five-game loss to Kansas City. His suspect defense also reared its ugly head at an inopportune moment. With the Mets trying to preserve a one-run lead in the eighth inning of Game 4, a slow grounder snuck under his glove—allowing the tying run to score and setting the stage for the winning runs to come home shortly after.

Nonetheless, Murphy was hailed as a Mets postseason legend. But it didn't take very long before he wasn't a Met anymore.

Less than a week after the World Series, the team presented Murphy a one-year, $15.8 million qualifying offer to remain in New York. No player had accepted such an offer in the short time this system had been in place. Murphy certainly wasn't going to be the first. He had every intention of leveraging his October performance into a more lucrative contract. It was not at a price that the Mets were willing to pay.

By not offering him a deal worthy of his escalated value, the Mets forced Murphy to look elsewhere. What he found was a team offering more years, more money, and the opportunity for vengeance.

Rebuffing the Mets' modest proposal, Murphy signed with the division rival Washington Nationals. He immediately made his old team pay more than they ever dreamed of. Within a year, he had transformed from Mets savior to Mets antihero.

During a 2016 season in which he was runner-up for NL MVP, Murphy torched his former club—batting .413 with 31 hits, seven homers, and 21 RBIs in 75 at-bats. He took it a little easier on them in 2017, *only* hitting .354 and driving in 14 runs. Murphy moved on to the Cubs and then the Rockies, and New York fans couldn't have been more relieved.

It's possible the Mets felt what he did at the end of 2015 was nothing more than an exaggerated product of a new pull-happy hitting mentality. That swing began its development in the Mets organization nearly a decade earlier, when it initially caught the eye of Steve Barningham. Murphy impressed the Mets scout with his ability to make contact and spray hits to all fields.

Barningham scoped out talent in northern Florida and believed he had found a hidden gem at Jacksonville University. But scouting directors, fixated on players who fit cookie-cutter profiles, were reluctant to take a player who had few strengths apart from the label "professional hitter."

There were 393 players taken in the 2006 draft before the Mets caved in and took Murphy in the 13th round. A little more than two years later, an injury to Marlon Anderson necessitated his call-up from the minors. Murphy wasted little time in confirming Barningham's wisdom, with 10 hits in his first 20 at-bats and batting .313 in 49 games.

He adapted quickly at the plate, but not on defense. The Mets experimented with Murphy in left field at the outset of his career, to very little effect. *The Hardball Times*, foreseeing the future, called him "a DH trapped in a left fielder's body."

Hitting was what Murphy did best. Doubles, specifically. His 38 in 2009 initiated a streak of at least 37 two-base hits in five of the following seven years.

He likely would have eclipsed that number in his other two seasons had not injuries prevented it. On March 30, 2010, Murphy hurt his right knee in a spring training game, prompting a rehabilitation which would last into early June. The rehab stint hit a serious snag while playing for the Triple-A club on June 2, when he suffered a high-grade MCL tear while trying to turn a double play. Although no surgery was required, it was a four- to six-month setback. Murphy avoided any serious harm for a good portion of 2011. Through 125 games, he had the third-highest batting average in the NL, but *another* MCL tear (this time to the left knee) brought his season to an abrupt end.

Murphy recovered nicely by 2012. Now permanently at second base, he became one of the best hitters at his position. He hit .291, and his 166 hits with 40 doubles established new personal bests. Murph missed just five games that year and only one the following season. Although his 2013 batting average didn't improve (.286), he was second in the NL with 188 hits. Murphy also contributed 13 home runs—a career high at the time—as well as 78 RBIs. And as wayward as Murphy could be on the base paths, he showed he was the league's most efficient base stealer, swiping 23 bags at an 88.4 percent rate.

While the Mets were making no headway in the standings, Murphy was carving out a reputation as a reliable bat, even if his fielding left much to be desired. From 2012 to 2014, he averaged over 15 errors—not including head-scratching on-field judgments that don't make the stat sheet.

Luckily for Murphy, this had little effect on his status as a second baseman. Case in point, the 2014 All-Star Game—the first of Murphy's career and the only appearance he'd make in a Mets uniform. At the time he was announced to the team, he had already surpassed 100 hits. By year's end, he'd reach 172 while batting .289.

Murphy's run of durability was impacted in 2015. He missed 32 games, most of them in June. About a month after his return, the lineup was revitalized with the addition of cleanup hitter Yoenis Céspedes, whose power rubbed off on Murphy. As New York headed toward the first division title of Murphy's Mets tenure, the 30-year-old drilled nine homers in the second half to give him a new career best of 14. But this certainly wasn't an indication of what was to come that October—a turn of events that was a complete aberration relative to the rest of his Mets career. And a career which, by then, was considered a success.

Murphy's bat control and assurance at the plate over seven seasons in New York would've granted him consideration for inclusion as an all-time team second baseman. The two-week power exhibition in October 2015, though, solidified his spot.

RESERVE SECOND BASEMAN—WALLY BACKMAN

Grace and elegance never won a game in his mind. Wally found whatever means necessary to get on base: walk, hit by pitch, drag bunt, infield single. Every aspect of his play was done with gritted teeth. Every at-bat, steal, or groundball was treated as if it would be the last. For Backman—who experienced call-ups, demotions, starting assignments, and bench roles—you can understand why. It made him a favorite among Mets fans and an agitator among Mets opponents.

The terms "gamer" and "throwback" are hackneyed and overused. But with Backman, they fit. Statistics don't properly convey how he shaped the image of the Mets teams he was a part of. Undersized but never overwhelmed, he galvanized others to perform beyond their potential.

"He was always the smallest guy on the field with the biggest heart," Ron Darling said. "It was a pleasure playing with him. He inspired everybody. If he could play that hard, why couldn't everyone else?"

Backman couldn't afford a let up. From the first season to the last, his status on the Mets roster was constantly in flux. It never had an adverse effect or served as a distraction from the manner with which he approached whatever task was given to him.

September 2, 1980, marked the major-league debut for both he and fellow prospect Mookie Wilson. Wally's one-month trial included a .323 batting average and a .396 on-base percentage in 110 plate appearances. He had made a case for inclusion on the Opening Day 1981 roster.

Backman made the team, but primarily as a pinch-hitter. Gold Glove Award recipient Doug Flynn had a firm grip on the starting second baseman spot, and an overall infield surplus kept Backman waiting.

The wait ended in 1982, when Flynn became a Texas Ranger. Backman was deemed worthy of the starting job with an OPS+ that matched All-Star catcher John Stearns for the team lead. But shoddy defense—14 errors in 88 games—prompted doubts about his staying power.

A broken collarbone ended Backman's season in mid-August, and it ushered in a new starter with a far better glove. Brian Giles unseated Backman and forced Wally's banishment to Triple-A. It would be a fortuitous demotion. His manager at Tidewater was Davey Johnson, who manned the same position for most of his 13 big-league seasons.

"I actually saw a lot of myself in him," Johnson said.

It would be a turning point in Wally's career.

"He saw what I could do and had confidence in me," Backman said. "That took a lot of the pressure off. I could relax and play my game."

While his batting average stayed safely above .300, his defense showed tremendous growth under Johnson's guidance.

"In the field, he showed me how to anticipate situations and showed me what I'd been doing wrong on the double plays," Wally said.

By 1984, Backman had demonstrated he was ready to return to the majors. Luckily for him, so was Johnson. As he took the managerial reins of the Mets, Davey remained impressed with Wally's penchant to punch above his weight, which couldn't be said for Backman's competition.

"[Brian Giles] had twice the talent—good speed, good power, good arm, smooth—but his makeup wasn't half as good as Backman's," Johnson said. "Wally would be our starting second baseman coming out of spring training. It was an easy decision for me."

Backman proceeded to validate that decision. He committed just 10 errors in 1984, and his .989 fielding percentage in 1985 was tops among National League second basemen. Wally augmented his improved defense over that two-year stretch with 62 steals and 264 hits (52 of which went for extra bases). He also made his mark in selfless contributions that don't get the glory in the box scores, like his league-leading 14 sacrifices in '85. But management still wasn't sold on him being an everyday player.

Backman had hit a measly .122 against left-handed pitching (as opposed to .314 versus righties). Thus, the decision to trade for right-handed Tim Teufel, once the second baseman in Minnesota, was born out of Johnson's assertion that switch-hitting Backman would benefit from almost exclusively facing right-handers. This enabled Wally to enjoy his best season in 1986. Serving as one half of a two-headed sparkplug alongside outfielder Lenny Dykstra, he batted .320, posted an on-base percentage of .376, produced 14 more sacrifice hits, and had a hand in 80 of the Mets' 108 wins.

Backman turned the ignition on in two game-winning drives to beat Houston in the NLCS. His ninth-inning leadoff drag bunt with the Mets down by a run in Game 3 paved the way for Lenny Dykstra's one-out homer to become a walk-off. The bunt rolled directly to Astros first baseman Glenn Davis, but Backman's speed out of the left-handed batter's box and his avoidance of Davis's tag allowed him to reach first base safely.

In Game 5, tied in the 12th inning with one out, his sharp grounder ricocheted off third baseman Denny Walling for an infield single. Backman moved into scoring position when reliever Charlie Kerfeld uncorked an errant pickoff attempt. Two batters later, he scored the game-winner on Gary Carter's single that handed New York a 3-2 series edge.

The next day, Backman was on the other end of a key run-scoring play. After entering for Teufel in the top of the ninth of Game 6, he delivered a 14th-inning pinch hit to bring Darryl Strawberry home and put the Mets ahead momentarily. Houston fought back to tie on Billy Hatcher's homer. Backman

It was rare to see Wally Backman without his uniform dirty. He defined grit on the 1986 Mets.

walked and scored in the 16th on a run that turned out to be valuable insurance, as the Astros rallied to within one before Jesse Orosco closed out an incredible 7–6 victory.

Just as they did in the LCS, Backman and Teufel platooned in the World Series, with Teufel penciled into the batting order to begin Games 1, 5, and 7 against Boston lefty Bruce Hurst and Wally in the lineup versus Red Sox right-handers. Backman hit safely in each his four starts and scored the tying run of Game 7's victory as a pinch-runner.

That winter, the Mets rewarded their scrappy second baseman with a new contract of roughly $3 million. Backman took on the burden of trying to live up to the lucrative new deal. The self-induced pressure had its consequences. His on-base percentage dropped 69 points and his batting average fell to .250 during an injury-shortened 94-game season.

"I was trying to pull the ball," he said. "I had just signed the three-year deal, and I felt guilty because I wanted to make up for it. You try to do things and you take away from your strength."

With 1987 a lost year, Wally sought to reset in '88. But he'd have to pass Teufel on the depth chart. His previous struggles led to a demotion that actually didn't last long. Teufel's injured hand in mid-May allowed Backman to rediscover his stroke. During a second half when the Mets pulled away with another division title, Wally hit .326 and reached base at a 41 percent rate. But this reemergence to the starting lineup would also be short-lived. The organization had anointed minor-league standout Gregg Jefferies as a cornerstone of the Mets' future. Backman's blistering September did nothing to change that. He reluctantly understood his days as an everyday player in New York were numbered in the face of a revered phenom like Jefferies.

Not even another clutch postseason moment—an eighth-inning game-tying double against the Los Angeles Dodgers, which led to an 8–4 Mets win and a 2-1 series advantage—could save him.

Wally was eventually shipped to Minnesota, traded for three nondescript prospects.

The separation didn't benefit either party. The 1989 Mets glaringly lacked Backman's fire. Wally, meanwhile, hit just .231 for the Twins and was released at season's end. He made brief and unremarkable stays with the Pirates, Phillies, and Mariners before calling it quits in 1993.

Wally believed his baseball acumen and swashbuckling attitude could translate into managing. Minor league teams agreed. Within five years post-retirement, he was in the dugout and didn't wait long after that to discover favorable outcomes. But the road to major-league managing proved tougher than his ambition to reach the majors as a player—himself being the primary impediment. Backman seemed to find his holy grail when he was hired as skipper of the Arizona Diamondbacks, only to be fired days later after reports surfaced about legal issues he had failed to disclose.

That devastating setback, along with others through the years, haven't destroyed his resolve. Even as his opportunities for another chance in the majors dwindle—including a denial from the Mets—Backman's renowned determination likely hasn't.

5

THIRD BASEMEN

STARTING THIRD BASEMAN—DAVID WRIGHT

Onto the Citi Field turf he ran, with the same hustle and spring in his step that he showed when he entered the Shea grounds for his debut 14 years earlier. He still flashed that same smile fans were so accustomed to.

On September 28, 2018, Wright said goodbye to a New York audience that watched him grow up before its eyes. But beyond the standing ovations, the tears, the thank-yous, and the recounting of great performances and records, a bittersweet feeling lingered.

Wright holds nearly every meaningful Mets hitting record. He's the all-time leader in at-bats and has played the second most games in orange and blue. There's a strong case for Wright being the greatest position player the team has ever had, with a 50.4 WAR that's second only to Tom Seaver.

But David Wright got cheated. His body betrayed him. It happens to some. It doesn't usually happen to the extent with which it hindered Wright in the prime of what was bound to be a Hall of Fame career.

From draft day to retirement day, he was tethered to this organization. For many Mets fans, this would be a dream. For

Wright, it was a dream come true. David grew up in Chesapeake, Virginia, far from Queens though close to the Triple-A affiliate in Norfolk.

But the fantasy wouldn't have played out if not for Bobby Bonilla. Yes, the Bobby Bonilla deferred payment that is derided annually every time the calendar hits July gave the Mets the money to sign free agent pitcher Mike Hampton. When Hampton left for Colorado after the 2000 season, the Mets were given a compensation draft pick the next year, and that pick happened to be Wright. Maybe July 1 isn't such a bad day after all.

Wright never gave the organization any reason to doubt he was a superstar-in-waiting as he excelled through the minor-league system.

July 21, 2004, marked the beginning of the end to the Mets' four-decade pursuit to stop the virtual revolving door at the hot corner. The necessary tools—in play and in presentation—to become the third base stalwart and team leader were readily present. Albeit a small sample size containing 69 games and 263 at-bats, Wright finished the year with a .293 batting average, 14 home runs, and 40 RBIs while carrying himself in a manner unusual for a 21-year-old.

Too often, highly regarded prospects succumb to the pressures of New York. Skills diminish before they truly flourish, and strong character weakens under the city's searing heat. With Wright, there was nothing to worry about.

As he entered his first full season (and shortstop José Reyes his second), new GM Omar Minaya added veteran pieces—most notably Carlos Beltrán and Pedro Martínez—around their two blue chips. The signing of Beltrán specifically allowed Wright the chance to mature as a hitter without too much pressure. But as a weary Mike Piazza—in his final Mets season—showed he was less formidable, and Beltrán couldn't get on track, Wright was among the few who kept the 2005 Mets steady amid a wild card chase. He led the team with 102 RBIs, 42 doubles, along with 27 homers. His .306 batting average was the eighth best in the NL and the first of five straight .300-plus seasons.

With Carlos Delgado and Paul Lo Duca in the fold for 2006 and another year for the prized left side of the infield to develop, the Mets were poised for greatness. During the regular season, that's exactly what happened.

New York was on its way to a division title, while Wright was on his way to becoming the best third baseman in the game. All-Star Games, many of them, were thought to be in his future shortly after he became a major leaguer. His first came at PNC Park in Pittsburgh. With an absence of nerves, Wright drilled a homer in his first at-bat. That came one night after thrilling the Steel City crowd with an abundance of long balls in a runner-up showing at the Home Run Derby. David was one of two NL players to hit at least .310 with 25 homers, 116 RBIs and 40 doubles that year, but his second half revealed a severe power outage. Many believed that the derby negatively affected his level swing, as he hit only four home runs after July 29.

He had just one more in the postseason. Wright batted .216 in his first venture into the playoffs. Despite the disappointing loss to St. Louis and Wright's uncharacteristic 4-for-25 performance at the plate, it seemed certain—especially with Reyes alongside him in the infield—there would be more Octobers in the offing. It didn't happen that way, but not for lack of effort on David's part.

By all historical and logical measures, the Mets had the 2007 NL East title sewn up. But not even a seven-game lead

Despite ravaging injuries that shortened his career, nobody has taken more at-bats or recorded more hits as a Met than David Wright.
DWONG19/DREAMSTIME

with 17 to play was safe. The seams burst over the final three weeks and playoff hopes withered away.

Next year came a smaller lead but the same result: another season-ending loss to the Marlins (which also turned out to be the closing day for Shea Stadium).

There is plenty of blame to go around for these consecutive collapses, none of which should be directed at Wright, who maintained MVP caliber while the fate of his team took a downturn.

Combining the Septembers of '07 and '08, David hit .330, averaged six homers and 21 RBIs, and preserved an on-base percentage of better than .420 and an OPS of about 1.000.

Over that full two-year span, arguably the best in Wright's career, he totaled 63 homers, drove in 231, batted .313, and reached base more than 40 percent of the time. The 2008 season was particularly productive. Wright posted a career high in homers (33), had at least 40 doubles for the fourth straight year, and the 124 RBIs he accumulated were a single-season club record.

The Mets were now building around Wright. But their new stadium didn't get the memo. Although David christened Citi Field with the Mets' first home run, future round-trippers were sporadic at best. The dimensions severely penalized right-handed power hitters, and they especially hurt the team's biggest star. Wright could only manage five homers at Citi in 2009 (as opposed to the 21 he hit at Shea in '08). He had just 10 total. Those faraway fences (since moved in) also played a role in his strikeout number, which reached an alarming 140.

The cavernous layout of Citi Field wasn't the only misfortune that permeated Queens in the first year of their new park. In a year marred by the team's financial ruin, injury, and disappointment, the typically durable Wright found himself on the disabled list for the first time—the result of a rising fastball to the helmet during an at-bat against San Francisco's Matt Cain. He was batting .324 at the time of the August 15 beaning. He returned two weeks later with post-concussion symptoms and hit only .239 for the balance of the season, deflating his batting average to .307.

Wright remained as stand-up a person as ever. He spoke with tact on behalf of the team in good times and in bad. Always a company man, Wright never threw anyone under the bus even when it would have been very easy to do so. And through this trial by fire, he became the de facto leader in the clubhouse—a role that would only grow in stature.

As the Mets sank deeper into mediocrity, he was the reliable star fans could cling to. In 2010, despite a higher strikeout rate (161 K's) and the lowest batting average since his rookie year, he regained his power stroke and hit out 29 while driving in 103 (the fifth time he eclipsed 100 RBIs).

Two years later, in 2012, the culmination of Wright's steady and stellar production manifested itself as team records. First, on April 25, he passed Darryl Strawberry for most RBIs. Then, on September 26, he became the Mets' all-time hit leader.

That offseason, the organization showed they were as faithful to David as he was to them. This had been a franchise that shied away from long-term contracts to players in their 30s, but Wright was a special case. A seven-year contract extension worth $138 million almost ensured him "Met-for-life" status. Wright was richer and more distinguished. He would later be named team captain, just the fourth in Mets history.

Dependability had been one of Wright's signature traits. From 2005 through 2010, he played in 935 of the Mets' 972 games. Seeing him man third base and bat in the heart of the Mets order had become a summer ritual in Queens. There was little reason to think his May 2011 lower-back stress fracture, which kept him out for two months and derailed any hopes of a productive year, was anything but an aberration. The way he played in 2012, with 21 homers, 93 RBIs, and a .306 average in 156 games quieted any concerns.

By all measures, Wright was on pace to put himself among the very best of third basemen. But 2012 would be the last time he'd play in at least 135 games. From there, fans were left to enjoy Wright in small doses.

Although he was healthy enough to participate heavily in the All-Star festivities in and around Citi Field in 2013, a right hamstring injury a month later held him to 58 RBIs for the year. A left rotator cuff contusion early in 2014 cost him a significant portion of his power. He hit only eight home runs.

But in 2015, while trying to recover from another hamstring issue, came the diagnosis that would ultimately derail him: spinal stenosis. In every practical sense, this narrowing of the spine was considered, at best, career threatening. But David was not about to let a pennant race go by without being an integral part of it.

When the leader of the Mets rejoined in August 2015, he homered into the upper deck in Philadelphia in his first at-bat. Then in a key September matchup with second-place Washington, Wright demonstratively fist-pumped upon scoring from first base on a double—which helped the Mets move closer to the division title. It was also fitting that in the first World Series contest at Citi Field, Wright provided the initial home run, a towering drive to left field in the first inning of Game 3.

After being granted the opportunity to remain healthy through another postseason run and his first Fall Classic, David's problems worsened. He could only get through 37 games of 2016 before his back flared up once more. Career mortality wasn't just nipping at his heels, it had him by the ankles. And it wouldn't let go.

With setbacks that likely would've forced a less determined player to give up, David was too steadfast to go out a broken man. But there was more than pride motivating him to make one final return. He wanted his young daughters—both of whom were born during his prolonged rehab—to get a chance to watch him play, in addition to getting one last opportunity to show his appreciation to New York.

By announcing he'd be in uniform for the final series of the 2018 season, Wright did go out on his terms. But those terms were severely altered by debilitating pain that barely allowed him to take the field again.

On that September 28 evening, with an anticipatory Citi Field sellout crowd there to say farewell, Wright charged onto the diamond alone to his customary spot at third base. He had to wave his teammates out to join him. One of them was Reyes, starting beside Wright for the 878th time, the most games together for any duo in Mets history and a poignant full-circle moment for a career which sadly veered off course before it could end in Cooperstown.

Loyalty can be hard to find these days. It's even harder to find in baseball.

Wright is securely placed with Seaver and Piazza as a pillar of this franchise. But no player better understood the passion of the fan base than he did.

"I live and die with this team," Wright said. "When I see the fans take losses hard, when I see the fans smiling from ear to ear after a win, I'm that same way in the clubhouse. And I'd like to think that that's what made this connection between the fans and me so strong, is that I relate to them, they relate to me, and we have similar feelings when it comes to the New York Mets."

Reserve Third Baseman—Howard Johnson

Some players have little trouble reaching major-league stardom—David Wright being a prime example. Some take a little longer before it all clicks.

Johnson had been a middling utility player in Detroit, fresh off a World Series title, when he was traded over to New York for starting pitcher Walt Terrell. His Mets tenure began similarly to his career as a Tiger, averaging a little more than 10 homers and 42 RBIs in his first two seasons while picking up another World Series ring.

But for the man they called "HoJo," his talents materialized in 1987. Granted the freedom to start with greater frequency, Johnson stunned baseball with a season highlighted by 36 home runs—24 more than he had hit in any previous year. If his sudden power turn was shocking, his penchant for speed on the base paths was equally an eyebrow-raiser. He stole 32 bases, outdistancing his career high by 22.

Johnson became the first Met to achieve a 30-homer, 30-steal season. And he'd do it twice more.

In 1989, Johnson matched his home run total of '87 and set a new personal best in steals with 41. Two years later, HoJo entered an exclusive segment of the 30-30 club. By knocking out an NL-best 38 and swiping 30 bases, he joined Bobby Bonds as one of only two players who had reached this rare single-season feat three times. By pacing the league in homers and RBIs, HoJo captured leadership in two-thirds of the National League's triple crown categories. The ascension of Johnson into the hitting elite contrasted his team's decline. As Johnson piled up the numbers, the Mets crumbled from their foundation.

Five years earlier, the roles were different—the player a still undiscovered commodity and the team on the verge of dominance.

But while HoJo occupied secondary status during the championship year of 1986, he played a significant part in helping the Mets set the tone in an early season battle with the St. Louis Cardinals.

All the bluster and bravado that exuded from New York would be hot air had it not taken care of the team they battled—and lost to—in a hotly contested NL East race in '85.

Benched in favor of a hot-hitting Ray Knight, Johnson entered on April 24 when the Cards brought in right-hander

Todd Worrell. Two outs from defeat, Johnson turned on a Worrell fastball and left no doubt about its end location. A long two-run homer in the ninth inning sparked New York to an eventual extra-inning victory.

Howard Johnson broke out in 1987, smashing 36 homers and stealing 32 bases. It would be the first of three 30-30 seasons.
JERRY COLI/DREAMSTIME

"Without question, that was a highlight of my career," he said. "I knew what it meant for our team and the lift it gave us."

The Mets went on to sweep the four-game set, and the Cardinals were never a factor in the NL East. They weren't alone, because the Mets used their 13-3 April as a springboard to a 21½-game spread over their nearest division competition.

The switch-hitting Johnson remained the left-handed option in a third-base platoon with Knight for a second straight year—nearly matching the production from 1985 despite playing in 38 fewer games. Yet a season with 10 homers, 39 RBIs, 54 hits, eight steals, and a .245 average wasn't going to convince anyone that he was about to take a significant stride forward.

Johnson made only seven plate appearances in the postseason and never reached base. He just so happened to be on-deck at the time of Mookie Wilson's Game 6 fateful grounder through the legs of Bill Buckner.

Knight, on the heels of winning World Series MVP, left the Mets for the Baltimore Orioles as a free agent, meaning Johnson was now the primary option at third base. No longer did Johnson have to be concerned with irregular playing time or worry about being benched if he ran into a slump. A refocused HoJo put in additional offseason work in a concerted effort to improve his right-handed swing.

After taxiing for a month, Johnson took flight in May. He hit five home runs that month, seven the next, and 10 in July. This stunning surge from a relative unknown gained national attention. But not everyone was convinced that this was the product of hard work or a clearer head.

Johnson went deep twice in a key series sweep in St. Louis—the second round-tripper prompting Cards manager Whitey Herzog to demand the umpires examine HoJo's bat.

Other suspicious skippers joined him: Montreal's Buck Rogers, Hal Lanier of the Astros, and the San Francisco Giants' Roger Craig—each of whom also had Johnson's bats confiscated on separate occasions. At no time was anything nefarious discovered.

With disbelievers brushed aside, Johnson swung and scurried his way into Mets history as the franchise's first 30-30 member. Darryl Strawberry joined shortly after, making them the first set of teammates to perform the feat in the same season.

This began a prolific five-year stretch highlighted by 157 homers, 475 RBIs, and 160 steals.

If only he could have transferred some of that production over to October. Despite his somewhat diminished stats in 1988, the Mets won the NL East again. But Johnson prolonged a deep playoff slump. His postseason hitless streak reached a record 22, which finally concluded in Game 5 of the NLCS. But his struggles still earned him a bench role for the final two contests. Johnson did get into Game 7 as a pinch-hitter and was struck out by Orel Hershiser—the last nail in New York's coffin as the destiny-laden Dodgers went on to a World Series title.

It was a fitting end to a year in which Johnson could never find the groove he enjoyed the season before. Likely too reliant on the long ball, HoJo popped 24 homers, but his .230 average and 68 RBIs were more telling.

By the end of '88, the Mets tried to squeeze more offense into the lineup at the expense of defense. In the playoffs, Wally Backman was slotted at second base, rookie Gregg Jefferies at third base, and Johnson at shortstop. The infield logjam caused by the emergence of Jefferies prompted Johnson's name to be thrown around in rumors and trade proposals—some of which nearly came to fruition.

The Mets were thankful they never pulled the trigger. With Backman gone and Jefferies now the everyday second baseman, HoJo was back starting at third, though he struggled mightily with throws across the diamond.

Johnson straightened those throws, the trade winds calmed, and he overcame his customary slow start to become the most valuable member of the lineup. While the Mets were largely a disappointment in 1989, Johnson certainly was not. Thanks to the retirement of Mike Schmidt combined with his own gaudy statistics, HoJo turned a stellar first half into an All-Star start.

Johnson would go on to establish both personal and franchise records. His 80 extra-base hits were the most by any Met, later tied by Carlos Beltrán in 2006 and broken by Pete Alonso in 2019. But he continues to stand alone in terms of single-season OPS+ (169) and offensive WAR (8.0).

Johnson had now established a pattern of a giant step forward followed by a small step back, and 1990 did nothing to alter that pattern. HoJo managed 23 homers and 90 RBIs, but his average took a 43-point tumble. He also moved over to play shortstop from early August through the rest of the season once starter Kevin Elster injured his shoulder—instigating a positional shuffle that would become a subplot of sorts during his later years as a Met.

But most of the discussion surrounding him in 1991, as it was in '87 and '89, was HoJo's rare offensive blend. One who is fleet of foot isn't normally a power threat, and a player with power doesn't usually run the bases well. That's what makes 30 home runs and 30 stolen bases in the same season so distinguished. To do it three times is to be part of an even more exclusive group.

Johnson did it with added emphasis, becoming the first Mets hitter to lead the National League in homers and RBIs in the same season, the third Met to hit more than 30 homers in three different seasons, and the third to post multiple 100-RBI years. Almost as impressive was the way he kept himself immune to the dissension and ailments that engulfed the Mets in the waning months of the schedule.

On top of that, Johnson spent a good portion of the second half in right field. He didn't seem to mind another position switch, but his feelings changed when he was asked to play center field at the start of the 1992 season.

"At 31, it was a little late for me to be learning a new position," Johnson said post-retirement. "Shea Stadium is a huge outfield, and I was drained every night. I constantly worried about all the ground that needed to be covered."

But position swaps were the least of Johnson's on-field concerns. His home run total underwent a steep reduction—down to just seven round-trippers. The Mets, too, plummeted to irrelevance.

The 1993 season wouldn't get any better. New York was on its way to a major-league worst record while HoJo discovered a multitude of ways to get on the disabled list. He suffered from an acute viral syndrome during the first half and endured a season-ending right thumb injury on July 22 when he slid head-first into second base. It was also the end to his Mets career. What limited action he saw during his swan song year in New York was a far cry from his prime seasons. Johnson struggled to get around on the fastball like he did before—contributing to a .238 batting average, seven homers (again), and 26 RBIs in 235 at-bats.

HoJo's best years came while the Mets were underachieving or, sometimes, worse. It's for that reason Johnson doesn't get enough consideration when discussing the franchise's best offensive players. But with the fourth-highest home run total (192), the fourth-most RBIs (629), and the third-most stolen bases (202), he deserves mention among such company.

RESERVE THIRD BASEMAN—ROBIN VENTURA

With some players, it's difficult to determine their signature moment. For Ventura, it's undeniable: the bottom of the 15th inning in Game 5 of the 1999 NLCS, bases loaded, one out, score tied at three.

A productive at-bat would extend the Mets' series with the Atlanta Braves and send the Shea Stadium crowd, soaked from a long bout of steady rain and sapped from a tension-filled near-six-hour epic, into exaltation.

A hit, a walk, or a sacrifice fly would've done the job. Before Ventura swung his bat on the fourth pitch from reliever Kevin McGlinchy, this game had already been cemented as a postseason classic. What followed, forever remembered as the "Grand Slam Single," became ingrained in Mets folklore and created one of the most unusual outcomes of all the October thrillers.

It's Ventura's signature play, but only because of its rarity and the drama that preceded it. His hit and subsequent attempt to circle the bases was an exclamation point on an epic chapter. The overall book on Ventura as a Met was short on time but not short on thrills. He compressed several moments into just three seasons in New York while defying a common and unpleasant occurrence.

From Vince Coleman to Bobby Bonilla to Jason Bay, Mets history is littered with catastrophic free agent fumbles. Ventura, wrestled from the White Sox in the winter of 1998, instantly proved to be a worthwhile investment.

Ventura came east already stocked with collegiate, national, and American League accolades. He led Oklahoma State to a pair of College World Series appearances and set a still-standing NCAA record with a 58-game hitting streak in 1987. A year later, Robin got the Golden Spikes Award as the best college player in the country and then helped Team USA take gold at the Summer Olympics.

As the occupant of the South Side's hot corner for much of the 1990s, he collected five Gold Gloves, surpassed the 30-homer mark once, and topped the 100 RBI plateau twice. In 1999, Ventura continued to be a premiere fielder in the National League, rewarded with Gold Glove number six. But it was his offense that made his first season in New York so essential and so significant to the Mets' cause. He established career highs in batting average (.301), slugging percentage (.529), OPS (.908), hits (177), and RBIs (120). His 38 doubles matched his previous best, and the 32 homers were just two less than his top total. When the NL MVP voting was tallied, Ventura was sixth—receiving more votes than teammate Mike Piazza.

During a two-month stretch in which the Mets dug themselves out of an early season hole and went 40-15, Ventura hit .337 with 16 home runs and 48 RBIs. But in late September, the Mets were teetering on disaster. Seven consecutive losses put them two back of Cincinnati and Houston in the NL Wild Card standings. New York, for all intents and purposes, needed a sweep of the Pittsburgh Pirates in the final regular-season series if it wanted to entertain thoughts of playing beyond the 162-game schedule.

Robin rescued the Mets in the opener—not once, but twice. New York took an early lead on Ventura's 32nd homer.

Robin Ventura used the phrase "Mojo Risin'" as a rally cry. He rose to the occasion often during a spectacular 1999 season.
JERRY COLI/DREAMSTIME

The Pirates tied it at one and sent it to extras. In the bottom of the 11th, with no place for the Bucs to put him, Ventura delivered a game-winning single to right-center.

The next night presented another must-win situation and another key hit from Robin, this time a bit earlier. With two on, Ventura laced a double down the right-field line to kickstart a 7–0 win. The Mets fulfilled their obligation, advanced past Cincinnati in a one-game wild card tie-breaker and into the playoffs.

But his considerable exploits came at a price. Battered and bruised, Ventura's weary body betrayed him over the course of a miserable postseason. But any pain that caused a .154 batting average was alleviated on October 15, with the Mets desperately trying to stave off elimination by the Atlanta Braves for the second straight night. In a nerve-racking NLCS Game 5 struggle that would turn into the longest postseason contest ever, Bobby Valentine made a host of strategic moves. But it's one he didn't make that proved most beneficial in the end.

"There were about five times I thought about taking him out of the game," the Mets skipper said. "He kept saying he could go."

Ventura managed an ordinary single in the 11th—his first hit of the entire postseason. Four innings later, after the Mets rallied from down 4–3 to tie it, came the extraordinary. Ventura stepped up with the bases filled and perhaps an unusual sense of comfort. It was a scenario Ventura thrived on. Eighteen times in his 16-year career, he had hit grand slams. On May 20, he had done so in both ends of a doubleheader.

"It's different when the bases are loaded and the guy has already walked a guy," said Ventura, who had been 1-for-18 in the NLCS. "He can't really fool around and throw a bunch of pitches in the dirt. So I'm just trying to get a ball in the air so the guy can score."

With the count 2-1, Ventura drove the next pitch to deep right-center. Deep enough to certainly score the winning run. Then deep enough to clear the fence.

"He scalded that ball," said backup catcher Todd Pratt, fresh from his recent encounter with fame when he sent the Mets to the NLCS on a walk-off homer. "I knew we had won the game just the way the ball came off the bat. It was just classic for him to come through."

Five hours and 46 minutes since first pitch, the Mets were winners. But the winning margin was still unsettled. After Ventura touched and rounded first base, he incessantly waved off enthusiastic teammates so he could circle the bases. Except their exuberance overwhelmed his would-be home run trot. They mobbed Ventura before reaching second, and the human base path blockade kept him from completing his trip. But whether the final score read 4–3 instead of 7–3 was of little consequence.

"As long as I got to first base, I don't care," Ventura said. "It means we won."

Game 5 breathed life into the Mets. The last breath was taken two nights later, but not without another dramatic chapter. Ventura went 1-for-6 with a double as the Mets clawed back from an early 5–0 hole to take the lead twice—only to lose in 11 innings.

Ventura's World Series hopes faded in the sixth game of the LCS, just as they had with the White Sox in 1993. The hopes would be fulfilled in 2000, but Ventura's lineup presence wouldn't be as prominent in that season or the next.

The challenge for Ventura to maintain his 1999 output would have been daunting even when fully healthy. But the accumulation of injuries gave him little chance. Still recovering from offseason surgery on his knee and right shoulder, Ventura couldn't swing as comfortably as before, nor could he throw as sharply. It would be only 87 games before his shoulder flared up again and sent him to the disabled list. His average fell to .232, although he still managed 24 homers and 84 RBIs in 141 games.

The Mets avoided any eleventh-hour panic and eased into the postseason for the second straight year. But like last year, their third baseman wasn't at 100 percent.

As New York defeated the Giants and Cardinals in the National League playoffs, Ventura's contributions were few— yet still vital. He drove in two of the four runs in the Mets' NLDS clincher over San Francisco, then tallied three RBIs in Game 4 of the NLCS versus St. Louis, bringing New York one win from the pennant. In their lone World Series victory, Ventura homered at Shea against the Yankees.

Ventura's 2001 campaign did not lead to better health. His 108 hits represented a career low for a season in which he played at least 100 games. His power and run production continued to be limited—21 homers and 61 RBIs.

The Mets put an end to Ventura's brief Queens stint by dealing him across town to the Yanks. In only 444 games, he offered up a weight of memories and performances more substantial than many who stayed much longer. Proof of that came on September 28, 2008, when he donned a Mets jersey again as part of Shea Stadium's closing ceremony. Upon introduction, he emerged from an opening in the right-center-field fence—mere feet from the landing spot of the hit that will forever define his Mets career.

6

SHORTSTOPS

STARTING SHORTSTOP—JOSÉ REYES

Anybody who complains about the dullness of baseball never saw José Reyes at his peak. Echoing Dwight Gooden and Darryl Strawberry, fans were drawn to Reyes's magnetic presence. Watching him was all about anticipation—edge-of-your seat anticipation—eagerly awaiting what would transpire at the plate or on the base paths. He quieted concession stands and shortened the lines to the bathroom. With gazelle-like quickness, he could turn groundballs into singles, singles into doubles, and doubles into triples. Any base ahead of him was there for his taking. By the time his Mets career was done, he had shattered every meaningful speed merchant record.

Reminiscent of Mookie Wilson, the man who once held the steals and triples records, Reyes was cultivated as a homegrown talent. The Mets had every intention to keep their 19-year-old phenom, who they signed at age 16 out of the Dominican Republic, in Triple-A for the entirety of the 2003 season.

But a team dragged down by has-beens like Mo Vaughn and Roberto Alomar as well as a declining Mike Piazza was in dire need of an energy boost—not to mention a reason for fans to feel good about the future. José was called up to be that spark.

Reyes batted better than .300 and stole 13 bases in 69 games, but the excitement was muted in September, when less than three months into his major-league career, the young shortstop's season was ended by a sprained ankle. And it wouldn't be the last time Reyes's wheels underwent repair.

Persistent hamstring problems and a misguided position switch to second base following the signing of Japanese star Kaz Matsui threw the 2004 season for a loop. The Mets also tinkered with the way Reyes ran, which did nothing but stunt the development of the 21-year-old. Seeing action in only 53 games in '04, Reyes was having difficulty finding his way.

Under the guidance of new manager Willie Randolph, two things were clear: Reyes would play shortstop and bat leadoff. With those parameters laid out ahead of the 2005 season, Reyes was quite literally off and running. Missing just one game, he led all National Leaguers in stolen bases with 60 and all of baseball in triples with 17. Establishing himself as the Mets' everyday leadoff hitter still required plenty of trial and error, as Reyes walked only 27 times. Despite a team-best 190 hits, his on-base percentage lagged at .300. Nonetheless, he brushed aside rumblings about his durability and proved that the praise heaped upon him as a teenager was justified.

In 2006, the ascent continued. Reyes became one of baseball's brightest stars alongside third baseman David Wright. He once more led both leagues with 17 triples and topped all base stealers (as well as his previous personal best) with 64. But he developed even further as a hitter as he raised his average to .300, drove in 81 runs, and even belted 19 homers.

Several standout performances showcased his versatility: a three-homer game against Philadelphia, a five-hit showing

The Mets' most exciting player, José Reyes is their all-time leader in stolen bases and triples.

against the Braves, and a cycle versus Cincinnati. Reyes was the kindle to the Mets' fire. The likelihood of victory increased when their catalyst performed to his potential. In New York wins, José hit .329 and stole 42 bases (as opposed to .252 and 22 steals in Met defeats).

By July, the Reyes-Wright combination was touted as the duo for the next decade, and both found themselves in the All-Star Game. While Wright remained rather low-key, an embodiment of professionalism despite his age, Reyes best captured the spirit and flavor of a 2006 Mets team that had the NL East title in its grasp before August.

His enthusiasm, however, was perceived by opponents as arrogance. The exuberant on-field celebrations and arranged handshakes he often initiated earned the Mets ire across the National League. Whether it was truly enthusiasm or arrogance, it would prove to be the karmic backdrop for what was to come in the weeks and years ahead.

The 97 wins and an easy division title rang hollow when New York fell to the underdog St. Louis Cardinals in a seven-game LCS defeat. Reyes was held to three extra-base hits, three stolen bases, and a .250 average in his first postseason.

But paired with David Wright on the left side of the infield, Reyes fostered dreams of a championship in the foreseeable future. New York got close to the mountaintop in 2005, closer still in 2006. There was little reason to doubt they would get more cracks at the playoffs.

That sentiment was certainly upheld. Reyes paced the NL in steals for the third year in a row and set the Mets' single-season stolen base record in 2007 with 78. He notched 191 hits, doubling 36 times and tripling 12 times.

The Mets were on cruise control, poised to embark on more World Series aspirations, until those plans were abruptly halted by both the Phillies and themselves.

Reyes faltered as the regular season went down to the wire. He hit .208 in September, had an on-base percentage of .279, and was held to just five steals over the final month. New York dropped 13 of its last 20 to fall short of the playoffs.

Reyes continued adding records to his name in 2008. He surpassed Mookie Wilson to officially become the Mets' most prolific base stealer as well as franchise leader in triples. He also led the league for the third time in three-baggers with a personal high of 19. And for the only time in his career, Reyes eclipsed 200 hits for a season, which was also best in the NL.

But once more, the Mets sputtered in the home stretch and missed the postseason. Reyes was not nearly as culpable this time—hitting 3 of his 16 homers in September, driving in 12 runs, and stealing 10 bases.

Any chance of extending a spectacular four-year run dissolved in 2009. The Mets gamebreaker began to break down again. Reyes was lost in mid-May with a right calf strain. Hopes for his return dwindled with continued setbacks in his rehab.

The lost time made it hard to shake the rust off in 2010. Reyes had the look of a player still trying to regain his rhythm. He stole just 30 bases and walked on 31 occasions but did manage to attain at least 10 triples for the fifth time.

Despite increasing fragility, Reyes remained a sought-after commodity if he felt the need to pursue free agency after the 2011 season. There was plenty of incentive, and he played like it early. On his way to an All-Star start, he maintained a batting average better than .300 after April 10 and racked up 15 triples by June 30. Two minor spells out of the lineup to repair his hamstring did nothing to slow his pursuit of the batting crown. As he continued to hold on to his high average, lead the NL in triples for a fourth time, raise his OPS to a career-best .877, and tally 39 stolen bases, Mets fans pleaded with the club to re-sign him.

The matter was still undecided heading into the regular-season finale, as were Reyes's batting title chances. But this game, which turned out to be José's last as a Met for five years, was bittersweet. With a two-point edge over Ryan Braun, Reyes executed a first-inning bunt single that all but assured him the league's top average. To lock it in, he immediately exited the game before Mets fans could celebrate him as the franchise's first batting champion.

It was a discomforting end to an electrifying nine-year stretch, as New York's effort to retain Reyes in the offseason was tepid at best. They not-so-grudgingly conceded to the Marlins, eager to bring fans to their new stadium, who were willing to pony up more money than a Mets franchise still feeling the effects of the Bernie Madoff scandal.

In nine seasons, he compiled a .292 average, 370 stolen bases, 99 triples, and 735 runs scored and a lengthy catalog of injuries that make his totals even more impressive.

Reyes discovered the grass wasn't greener in South Beach, Toronto, or Denver. With three unremarkable stops in five years, it was understandable to hear Reyes longing to return to his first baseball home.

"I'd love to finish my career here in New York," he said while a member of the Rockies in 2015. "I have some great memories here."

The fans agreed. When he came back to Citi Field that year, the crowd gave him a standing ovation—a unanimous sign of approval. That eventually changed because, while Reyes made his way back to Queens in July 2016, his arrival was not without baggage. A domestic violence charge was trouble he couldn't outrun. With a damaged past and an uncertain future, some now didn't even want him there—and justifiably so. The Mets signed him anyway, with excitement less fervent and reputation slightly tarnished.

Much of the tread had worn from the tires that made him among the most dynamic Mets position players—far from the player who averaged 195 hits and 64 steals from 2005 to 2008. And as 2016 turned to 2017, his talents faded further, although he did manage to move into second place on the Mets' all-time hits list.

By the time the 2018 season arrived, the 35-year-old Reyes had deteriorated almost beyond recognition. With baseball morticians on call, he finished with a meager .189 average and just 19 extra-base hits in 110 games.

It's tempting to put aside a rather forgettable second stint in New York and choose to remember the greatness of his initial nine-year stay—particularly, the recollection of an extra-base hit in the gap or a daring steal of third.

Reyes might not have fulfilled every promise hoped of him when he burst onto the major-league scene, but there's no regret when it comes to the thrills he supplied for the better part of a decade.

RESERVE SHORTSTOP—BUD HARRELSON

Don't be fooled by his 5-foot-11, 160-pound frame. Harrelson defined toughness. An athlete of greater stature might readily look the part of a major leaguer. Not Bud. He had to earn everything.

While Harrelson's limitations at the plate were undeniable—as a 16-year career batting average of .236 with seven home runs will certainly attest—his value as a fielder was tremendous.

The measurements for what constitutes a top-level shortstop vary with team and time period. Harrelson's importance wouldn't have been felt had he played on a club less dependent on pitching and defense. From the late 1960s through the mid-1970s, the Mets cherished a reliable glove as much as a potent bat. Harrelson's steadiness in the field was held in high esteem by those who benefited from it most.

"Having him playing at shortstop every day is like having a top-notch pitcher," said Tom Seaver. "It keeps you out of a losing streak."

Harrelson was the glue that kept the Mets infield together and the glove his pitchers could trust—finishing with a lifetime fielding percentage of .969. In 1970, he set a then-major-league record of 54 consecutive errorless games at shortstop—the same year as his first All-Star selection. He'd make the Midsummer Classic again as a starter in 1971 and ended the year with a Gold Glove Award.

But no acknowledgment of Harrelson would be complete without mention of the fight in the 1973 NLCS.

The origin of the dustup between Bud and Pete Rose occurred after Game 2, when Harrelson made self-deprecating, yet stinging, comments regarding Cincinnati's futile offense, saying, "They looked like me hitting out there." The Reds sought to get even in Game 3, and Rose was set to carry out that vengeance when he slid hard into Harrelson covering second base on an inning-ending double play. Bud instantly objected to the malice. Rose shoved. Harrelson shoved back. It was on from there. Both teams hustled to the scene. A few punches were thrown. Some uniforms were dirtied. Several feelings were hurt. But nobody was ejected.

The battles for Bud were far different nearly a decade earlier. Before fighting the likes of the hit king, Harrelson was simply fighting for major-league recognition.

Roster expansion at the back end of the 1965 season offered Harrelson room to debut on September 2 as a pinch-runner. He started the following year at Triple-A Jacksonville, but over the next three seasons, he forged three crucial relationships that would forever shape his career.

His Jacksonville Suns teammate in '66 was none other than Seaver, a fellow Northern Californian who became his roommate and longtime friend. Bud returned to the majors in mid-August, where he was taken under the wing of starting shortstop Roy McMillan. The veteran worked to correct defensive lapses that plagued Harrelson in the minors. McMillan's retirement presented Harrelson the chance to be an everyday player. Although he was second among National League shortstops in putouts and third in assists for 1967, Bud remained a work in progress. He committed 11 errors over his first 20 games, ending the year with a league-high 32 (which led to 23 unearned runs).

Like the Mets themselves, Harrelson sought additional guidance. It arrived in the form of new manager Gil Hodges. And it was under his leadership that Bud helped shed the Mets' reputation of inferior defense while subsequently solidifying himself as an elite defender. New York had the fourth-fewest errors in the league in 1968. Harrelson himself shaved his error total down to 15. Though he batted .219, the blemish of Bud's hitting limitations could be redeemed by how well he performed in the field.

That would only improve in the ensuing years.

As the Mets rose out of the pits and into prominence, Harrelson's outstanding glove work and significance to a team built on pitching and run prevention were gaining attention. In 1969, he began a four-year stretch in which he finished in the top five in fielding percentage among shortstops each year. Part of New York's near-flawless defense that October can be attributed to Harrelson. His only miscue in 44 postseason chances proved rather insignificant, occurring in the seventh inning of New York's 11–6 win over Atlanta in Game 2 of the NLCS. It was against the Braves that Bud produced his only two extra-base hits of the postseason and his only three RBIs. The runs he helped suppress had a considerable effect in that series and especially versus the Baltimore Orioles in a five-game World Series triumph.

Harrelson's best two years were ahead of him as he picked up in-season and end-of-season accolades along the way. While his defense stayed superior in 1970, his offense dispensed with its liabilities. Harrelson set multiple career highs, including runs scored (72), runs driven in (42), and walks (95). He stole 23 bases in 27 attempts after stealing just one in '69. Bud also homered for the first time since 1967 and showed additional muscle with 18 doubles, eight triples, and eight sacrifice flies.

The All-Star selection was an honor repeated the next year at Tiger Stadium—part of a starting lineup among power hitters like Hank Aaron, Willie Mays, Willie McCovey, Willie Stargell, and Johnny Bench. Bud's hitting in 1971, in comparison to his past, measured up well. His 138 hits bested his 1970 output by one, as did his 28 steals.

Harrelson's .252 batting average was his highest since 1967. But, as would usually be the case, his fielding stood out above everything else. And for '71, it stood out among other NL shortstops with the Gold Glove.

Bud's defense got the recognition it deserved, but the recent advent of advanced metrics have given additional enhancement to those merits. For instance, his fielding runs above average, which calculates how much a player is worth in terms of defensive plays made, was highest among all shortstops in 1971. Harrelson's range factor, determined by dividing putouts and assists by the number of innings, was twice best among shortstops (1967 and 1974).

It wouldn't be long before Harrelson's frailty couldn't stand the rigors of a full season. Bud missed 300 games over the next six years due to damaged hands, sternum, back, and knees. In none of those seasons did he play more than 118 games. And just once in that half-dozen-year period did the Mets return to the playoffs, which also happened to be the year his feistiness and unwillingness to back down gained notoriety.

Harrelson was swept up in the tidal wave of injuries that threatened to cast the Mets' 1973 season adrift. His presence—or lack thereof—in commanding the infield could be noticeably felt. During two separate stints on the disabled list, the Mets were 23-36. With Harrelson, they were 59-43. Luckily for New York, he was there when it mattered, and so were most other key contributors. Propelled once again by great pitching and sturdy defense, the Mets won 19 of 27 in September and took the NL East despite an 82-79 record.

Held hitless in the NLCS opener with the Reds, Harrelson produced a single and an RBI in a 5–0 win that evened the series. That was more than could be said for Cincinnati's entire Game 2 output. His pointed criticism of the Reds' offense served as the impetus for the melee that ensued in the fifth inning of Game 3. Umpires didn't see a reason to toss Rose or Harrelson from what had become a lopsided contest. The

Bud Harrelson was vital for the Mets' defensive-oriented mind-set from the late 1960s through the mid-1970s.
JERRY COLI/DREAMSTIME

closest either came to an early departure was when the Shea crowd pelted Rose with litter as he took the field in the inning following the fight. The insanity in the stands subsided enough for the continuation of the game—a 9–2 Mets win that put New York one victory from the pennant.

Rose's 12th-inning homer the next day extended the series to its limit, but the Mets prevailed—meaning a meeting with the defending champion Oakland A's. It offered Harrelson another chance to put his feisty demeanor on full display.

The Mets split in the Bay Area, but not without some Game 2 madness.

Harrelson prepared to score the go-ahead run in the top of the 11th on a Félix Millán flyball to left field. As Bud approached home plate, he resisted the slide and evaded the tag of catcher Ray Fosse. But umpire Augie Donatelli thought otherwise, prompting Harrelson and a cavalry of Mets to angrily dispute the judgment. As instant replay showed they had every right to vent their frustration, and since this was 1973 and not 2019, the Mets could only stew in their disdain—though not for long.

Harrelson began the top of the 12th with a double (his third hit in six at-bats), moved to third on Tug McGraw's bunt single, and scored on Willie Mays's single. The Mets added three more to prevail in what was, at the time, the longest game in World Series history.

New York won Game 2 but lost Game 7. It would be 13 years before the Mets made another playoff venture. Bud would be there for it, serving in a much different role.

By 1977, the Mets dispensed with beloved figures from the championship era. It was Harrelson's turn in the spring of 1978. He became a Philadelphia Phillie, then a Texas Ranger. But after retirement, Bud knew where his allegiances lay.

Not ready to sit idle, Harrelson served as coach, broadcaster, and minor league manager before moving back to the parent club as part of Davey Johnson's staff, where he became the only man to wear the orange and blue for both Mets championships. Harrelson got a firsthand perspective of the 1986 World Series and helped escort Ray Knight home from the third-base coaching box in the climax to Game 6. The Mets' successes led to tempting offers for Bud to manage elsewhere, but he wanted to lead the Mets. That patience was rewarded when Johnson was removed after a slow start to 1990.

The Mets were reignited under Harrelson's leadership, going 71-59 and tussling with the Pirates for the NL East flag before ultimately falling a few games short. The 1991 season appeared to follow a similar track. But as the Mets fell apart in July and lost games at a furious pace during the second half, Bud was unable to keep the pieces together. With a week still to play, he was put out of his misery.

Any negative sentiments stemming from his dismissal have long since dissipated. For the player who remains on the team's top-10 list in games played, at-bats, hits, triples, and stolen bases, it's only cheers. And those cheers have had special significance recently as Harrelson battles Alzheimer's disease, a diagnosis first received in 2016. But the magnitude of the opponent has never fazed him. As we've learned for more than a half-century, Bud Harrelson doesn't go down without a fight.

7

OUTFIELDERS

STARTING RIGHT FIELDER—DARRYL STRAWBERRY

He's the franchise's all-time home run king. He's first in adjusted on-base plus slugging, second in slugging percentage, and second in RBIs. The offensive section of the Mets record book is a literal Strawberry field forever.

But Darryl left us wanting more. With his smooth hitting motion, he belted out 252 homers and drove in 733 runs. With swift legs, he stole 191 bases. He made the All-Star team seven times. He contributed to the 1986 world championship club. Nevertheless, after eight successful seasons, there is an emptiness to his Mets career.

Strawberry deprived fans of added greatness. But in truth, he deprived himself of maximizing the wide array of skills at his disposal. He was fascinating and confounding. A man with limitless talent but limits in maturity. A player whose ability was weighed down by his baggage. For all his troubles, he remains the greatest power hitter the Mets ever produced and among the franchise's greatest players, but he should've been one of Major League Baseball's all-time greats.

It was those kind of expectations that surrounded Strawberry before the Mets made him the top overall pick in the

1980 amateur draft out of Los Angeles's Crenshaw High School. Darryl was tall and lean, blessed with a sweet name and a sweeter swing. A *Sports Illustrated* feature compared the 18-year-old Strawberry to Ted Williams. With a thoroughbred build and a swift upper-cut made for home runs, he had all the makings of the revered "five-tool player." Strawberry was not unlike other African American males who were raised in poverty-stricken households, where sports offered a chance to break away from the cultural and economic restraints imposed on them by their surroundings.

While baseball was sure to change that for Darryl, he began showing signs of immaturity while in the rookie-level Appalachian League. There were laments about his work ethic and late arrivals to the ballpark. Once he even missed an entire game. A player of a lesser status would've received a stern reprimand. But because of his promise, the absence was largely ignored. His talent was too good to discount.

On May 6, 1983, the Mets unveiled their shiny new toy in the MLB showroom. For a team already 10 games out of first place and not getting any closer, this was the sign of hope fans would cling to for the remainder of the season. Strawberry struggled mightily as he tried to adjust to baseball's top level. Over his first month, he hit .165 and struck out every 2.5 at-bats.

But after about five weeks, Strawberry began to figure it out. Beginning on June 7, Darryl fashioned an OPS of .936, topping the figure of NL MVP Dale Murphy. His power took a serious upturn in the second half as he hammered 19 homers and drove in 51 runs. By September, the glimpses of his potential were now on full display. In the final month of his Rookie of the Year campaign, he exhibited great plate discipline by batting .376 and hitting successfully in 20 of 24 games. His final totals of 26 homers and 76 RBIs stood as Mets rookie records until both were shattered by Pete Alonso in 2019.

The hope was that Strawberry would ascend further into superstardom. And while he improved in several offensive categories, the growth was incremental in most areas. In 1984, Darryl duplicated his rookie season's home run total, struck out nearly as frequently, and batted around the .250 mark. With Keith Hernandez and Wally Backman entrenched at the top of the lineup, Strawberry took advantage of his spot in the batting order by driving in 97 runs.

Torn ligaments in his thumb, the consequence of diving for a sinking flyball, kept Strawberry on the mend for all but 10 games in May and June of 1985. Darryl's on-field reputation earned him a second All-Star Game selection in as many years. It certainly wasn't his .225 batting average that did it. His blistering second half—which featured a 1.035 OPS and 60 RBIs—retroactively proved it was a wise choice.

On the afternoon of August 5 at Wrigley Field, Strawberry took Chicago Cubs pitching to task—with a rope to right-center and a pair to straightaway center. They were three of the 23 homers he'd launch over the season's final three months.

On the night of October 1 in St. Louis, his titanic 11th-inning blast went above the center-field stands and caromed off the Busch Stadium clock to give the Mets a 1–0 win and kept his team breathing in a frantic, yet futile, attempt to catch the Cardinals. Darryl did his best to try and stop time. Within a couple of days, though, the Mets ran out of it. The chase ended three games short.

But in 1986, everyone was chasing New York. Strawberry—clouting 27 homers and driving in 93—was one of several

Darryl Strawberry had talent equal to the greatest players ever. Although he never reached his full potential, he remains the Mets home run king and near the top of most hitting categories.
JERRY COLI/DREAMSTIME

contributors for a team where no player stood out and few players fell short. The Mets piled on the wins and added to their division lead, becoming the subject of intense media attention for their dominance and arrogance.

"We were different from everybody," Darryl recalled. "We had that swagger. We were vicious. We would fight with teams.... When we got between those lines, we were serious about kicking your behinds. It showed what a team is all about. We were unified and we cared about each other."

But in '86, it appeared the only care Strawberry had was about himself. The emotionally stunted youngster could be vicious and selfish. He took pride in making others feel inferior. Each commercial and music video seemed to enlarge his canyon-sized ego. All the while, he was routinely abusing drugs and drinking heavily. Under the MLB drug policy in place in the 1980s, no team could force a player to take a drug test. Winning masked any mayhem going on in the clubhouse. And with Davey Johnson as manager, who was never eager to castigate his players, nobody truly reined him in.

The white-hot spotlight made Darryl open to ridicule. This wasn't limited to opposing fan bases. Even the Shea faithful got on his case in August, when Strawberry failed to produce a hit at home for the entire month.

He rode out the rest of the season, then endured a turbulent postseason filled with tumult and triumph. His 12 strikeouts in the NLCS against Houston were offset by two clutch tying home runs that got the crowd back on his side.

New York chipped away at Bob Knepper's 4–0 lead in Game 3 with two hits and an error that brought in a run. Quivering Shea was waiting to burst. Strawberry wouldn't let them down. As Knepper tried to get ahead in the count with a first-pitch fastball, he didn't have the velocity to throw it by Darryl's quick bat.

Straw delivered again in Game 5. Nolan Ryan had retired the first 13 batters. Not the 14th. Darryl ended Ryan's hitless day—and the shutout—with a tracer that had enough height and hook to sneak over the fence in the right-field corner.

By the World Series, Strawberry was not just a big target but an easy one. Fenway Park took full advantage in Game 5 of the World Series. The Red Sox were in the process of sewing up a victory behind Bruce Hurst, giving the crowd a chance to turn its focus on the temperamental right fielder. A derisive "Daaarrrr-ylll, Daaarrrr-ylll" serenade lasted minutes and would follow Strawberry throughout his career.

But he had an answer in Game 7. Strawberry sent a towering drive over the right-center-field wall to lead off the bottom of the eighth—his first home run and first run batted in of the World Series—and gave the Mets breathing room in what would be an 8–5 win. Straw savored the moment—sauntering around the bases like there was nobody waiting for him—then fittingly provided one last curtain call in a year filled with them.

That homer washed away the scorn of two nights prior, when he was removed by Davey Johnson in the eighth inning of Game 6 on a double-switch and publicly shared his frustration with the media. Choosing the worst possible time for public outbursts became something of a habit for Darryl.

During the 1988 NLCS against Los Angeles, Strawberry hinted at the possibility of joining the Dodgers after his current contract expired. A few months later, he took out his frustration with Keith Hernandez by trying to physically fight him at team picture day amid the press corps. On top of that were routine accounts of loafing, lateness, and legal battles. This kept Mets fans in an emotional quandary, trying to balance cheers for his ability with condemnation of his indiscretions.

Such was the case in 1987. He attained personal highs in homers (39), RBIs (104), steals (36), along with batting average, on-base percentage, and slugging. But his statistical prowess was partially clouded by more pointed criticism of Johnson and a war of words with teammates Wally Backman and Lee Mazzilli after they questioned his desire to play (in favor of recording a rap album).

Strawberry began 1988 with a 4-for-4 day and two home runs. The second reached the nether regions of Montreal's Olympic Stadium, a ball that might have cleared customs if not for the roof. He'd hit 37 more to match his career-high total from '87 and lead the National League. He topped 100 RBIs for the second straight year and was one steal short of back-to-back appearances in the 30-30 club.

For the first time, Darryl was garnering serious consideration for Most Valuable Player, thanks in part to the Mets pulling away from their NL East competition in September and claiming their second division title in three years.

Yet it was the Dodgers' Kirk Gibson who took top billing over Strawberry (not to mention a World Series ring) later that fall. Gibson also had the upper hand when his Dodgers took on Darryl's Mets in the playoffs. While Strawberry hit .300, drove in six runs, and had a gargantuan homer in Game 4, Gibson delivered two key longballs in LA's seven-game upset.

Darryl was not the MVP in '88, but he was definitely the most volatile during spring training 1989 after his quarrel with Hernandez. That kind of fighting spirit was hard-pressed to be found during the season. Strawberry endured a sharp reduction to his batting average, down to .225, with barely more than 100 hits. He came up one short of another 30-homer season, and his 77 RBIs were the lowest since his rookie year.

The responsibilities increased entering 1990. With Hernandez and Carter now gone, this was officially Darryl's team.

In what would turn out to be Strawberry's swan song in Queens, it didn't go by quietly. Only this time, less talk and more action. Especially in June, when he batted .412 during an 18-game hitting streak, bashed 10 homers, and drove in 27. Behind Strawberry, the Mets advanced up the standings to counter a slow start—getting into first place in July before ultimately coming up three games short of Pittsburgh.

But his year was not shrouded in as much disappointment as '89. By driving in 108 runs, he set a single-season franchise record to go along with 37 homers and an .879 OPS. He was also among the top five outfielders in fielding percentage and the top five National Leaguers in WAR.

Strawberry made good on his recurring threats to explore free agency—thoughts that weren't completely taken seriously by teammates when they considered the source. He jetted for Los Angeles, leaving behind many thrills and controversies. But the troubles wouldn't leave him. Darryl's career continued to be marked by behavioral indiscretions that prevented what should've been easy entrance into the Hall of Fame.

Once the agent of his own demise, he now understands the human wreckage he caused. After years of turmoil and numerous arrests and conflicts, Darryl found enlightenment as an ordained minister and has since changed for the better. As for his legacy—a player who failed to fulfill the promise of his gifted abilities but still enjoyed his share of successes and accomplishments—that will never change.

RESERVE RIGHT FIELDER—RUSTY STAUB

There's a stereotype that redheads have an outwardly fiery temperament. But in the case of Daniel Joseph Staub, he was a gentle soul with a quiet intensity underneath. He ensured that each season, each game, and each at-bat had his utmost attention. That noted passion later translated into serving communities with the same commitment he gave on the field for over two decades. Throughout his career and his post-retirement life, Staub was a devoted native of two different regions, revered in two different countries, and cheered for in two different languages.

He had one distinguishing trait throughout his 23 major league seasons. Staub didn't become the first player to tally at least 500 hits with four different clubs by accident. He totaled 11,229 plate appearances over the course of a career that encompassed 2,951 games. Each entry into the batter's box was a self-indoctrination—a chance to apply all he did know and discern what he hadn't known before.

In a *New York Times* article, Rob Hoerburger wrote: "Decades before analytics became commonplace in baseball, [Staub] compiled the goods on every pitcher he faced in the batter's box or observed from the top step of the dugout: patterns, windups, motions, a tap of a cleat, an eyebrow twitch, any idiosyncrasy or quirk that might tip a pitch."

The scholarly Staub earned his baseball master's degree. Thanks to longevity and awareness of the strike zone, he reached base more often than Rogers Hornsby and Tony Gwynn and recorded more hits than Ted Williams and Joe DiMaggio. He got there more through diligence than natural ability.

"I discovered at a very early age that nothing was going to come easy for me, that I'd have to work for my success," he said. "And when I was successful, it was very rewarding because I knew how hard I had worked to get to that point."

Appreciation came easy in Montreal. After six seasons in Houston that featured two All-Star appearances, Staub was sent to the expansion Expos for 1969. Appreciation quickly evolved into adoration. Rusty embraced Montreal and learned to speak French. Montreal wasted no time embracing "Le Grand Orange."

But the locals were forced to let go in April 1972. Gil Hodges, shortly before his death, insisted on getting Staub to strengthen a weak Mets offense. The Expos agreed to part with Rusty in exchange for three youngsters. It was a turn of events Staub initially had trouble coping with.

"I handled it very professionally to a certain extent," he said. "But I never thought I'd be traded from there. I didn't know how great it was going to be for me when they did it. But when they moved me, it hurt me as a person."

Just as the trade was devastating to Montreal's fan base, New York reveled in getting a player of Staub's caliber—someone who could add spice to an lineup that was getting rather bland.

Staub, who had played well for perennial second-division clubs, fed off the talent around him and the Mets benefited from Rusty's arrival. New York jumped out by winning 25 of its first 32. Staub's insertion in the cleanup spot expanded the possibilities of the offense and lessened pressure on Tommie Agee and Cleon Jones. Combined with their usual supply of great pitching, the Mets were six games up on Pittsburgh by May 21.

The good times, though, would end abruptly.

Staub, hitting .315 with eight homers and 31 RBIs, was plunked on the right hand by a pitch from soon-to-be teammate George Stone of Atlanta on June 3. Although he tried to fight through the pain, the soreness was too much. X-rays disclosed a fractured hamate bone. It was part of an epidemic that engulfed the Mets, as Agee, Jones, and others were also set back by injuries. When Rusty went on the disabled list, the

Rusty Staub had two distinct periods with the Mets and served them well in both.
JERRY COLI/DREAMSTIME

Mets were perched in first place. When he came back on September 18, the Mets were 16.5 games out.

The start of the 1973 season charted an all-too-familiar and unwelcome pattern. Staub couldn't shake the injury that derailed his '72 campaign, while other vital members of the Mets succumbed to similar fates. Staub missed only 10 games but couldn't carry the Mets out of last place. With a little more than a month left in the regular season, they were still in the NL East cellar.

A grand slam on August 27 against San Diego helped to forge New York's resurgence. Staub stayed at the forefront by batting .321 with five homers, 21 RBIs, and 24 runs scored over the final 33 games. He ended on a 15-game hitting streak, going 4-for-5 with two runs scored and an RBI in a 6–4 NL East–clinching victory over the Cubs.

"It was the most together I've ever seen people get in my career," he later said. "We became a unit. It was one of the best periods of my life."

Staub's scorching bat kept blazing in the third game of the NLCS. Two home runs in two at-bats gave him three for the series and jump-started the Mets to a 9–2 victory that put them on the precipice of an unlikely pennant. Staub's offense decidedly won Game 3. His defense nearly won Game 4.

Rusty made an over-the-shoulder grab in the top of the sixth to preserve the Mets' slim 1–0 lead. Then in the 11th, Dan Driessen had what appeared to be a tie-breaking extra-base hit, but Staub raced back onto the warning track and hauled it in.

This valiant effort, though, was made in vain. As Staub secured the catch, he careened into the right-center-field wall. Though he pressed on through the Reds' 12-inning victory, a separated shoulder made him unavailable for the Mets' deciding fifth-game victory.

Staub's status remained in doubt heading into the World Series against Oakland. The designated hitter, introduced that regular season, was not implemented for the Fall Classic.

Manager Yogi Berra chose to sacrifice Rusty's limitations in the field for what he could do at the plate. Though he toughed it out, Staub's shoulder pain forced him to throw submarine style. It had no effect on his hitting, however. Staub batted .423 for the series, hitting safely in each of the six games he played. He drove in five of the Mets' six runs while belting a pair of homers in a Game 4 victory that helped New York draw even with the A's. But Staub's weary body could only take the Mets so far. Despite going 2-for-4 in the seventh game, driving in one of his team's two runs, New York produced little else in a 5–2 defeat that gave Oakland the title.

The Mets couldn't withstand another injury-riddled season. The setbacks and struggles of several key performers in 1974 had a ripple effect on Staub. Without much protection in a lineup that collectively batted .235, he experienced his lowest average and hit total since 1965.

Questions from management that offseason regarding his weight and stamina were proven unfounded the next year. With slightly better success at the front of the batting order, Staub took full advantage as he became the first Met to surpass 100 RBIs in a single season. A year like '75 would supposedly make him an indispensable piece to a team lacking in run-producing hitters.

Nonetheless, team chairman M. Donald Grant had a penchant for severe miscalculations. Planting seeds of public discontent that would grow in the coming years, Grant sent Staub to Detroit for a prospect and washed-up former World Series MVP Mickey Lolich.

The Mets were not dissuaded by a possible decline from Lolich and, likewise, were buying the stock of Mike Vail as a starting right fielder—after concluding his initial big-league stint with a .302 average and a 23-game September hitting streak.

The deal provoked instant seller's remorse. Vail ravaged his knee while playing basketball during the winter, which cost him a bulk of the '76 campaign, and he never returned to optimal condition. Lolich went 8-13 in his only season sporting a Mets uniform.

Staub, meanwhile, would enjoy his three most productive seasons. Little did Rusty know, he departed Queens just before the roof collapsed and came back, in 1981, as the moribund Mets were trying to regain mediocrity. The interlude between Mets acts added three more stops to his major-league itinerary: Detroit, Montreal once more, and then to Texas.

Upon arriving back in New York, Staub would be more mentor than mainstay. Now a restaurateur and gourmet cook, his indulgence had let his weight creep up to 240 pounds. He had sundial speed and modest power, but he still possessed that keen eye and a wicked encyclopedia of hitting knowledge. Mixing in occasional spells at first base and fewer turns in the outfield, Staub's primary job was pinch-hitter.

It became an ideal role for Staub in the twilight of his career. So much so that, in 1983, he led the majors with 24 pinch-hits, set a National League record for hits in consecutive pinch-hit at-bats with eight, and his 25 pinch-hit RBIs equaled an all-time record. Over his final four seasons, Rusty compiled 99 pinch-hits and drove in 92 runs.

In retirement, he maintained two Manhattan restaurants and took a turn in the Mets broadcast booth. More impactful, he established the New York Police and Fire Widows and Children's Benefit Fund in 1985, which provides ongoing assistance to the families of first responders through financial and emotional support—an effort that rose to prominence in the wake of the September 11, 2001, attacks.

Rusty Staub literally and figuratively touched all the bases. He addressed each of his many ventures—from baseball to dining to charitable causes—with similar dedication. Staub passed away in 2018, but in many respects, the fire still burns bright.

Starting Left Fielder—Cleon Jones

The 1969 World Series featured its share of unforgettable catches. There was the pair of sensational grabs from Tommie Agee in Game 3 and Ron Swoboda's sprawling dive to save Game 4. Jones, too, penned his signature play in the Mets' triumph over Baltimore. It wasn't memorable for its spectacular nature. It was notable because of its finality.

The catch that concluded New York's improbable journey to championship glory is among the team's iconic images. As he stepped back onto the warning track to reach his arms out, hold his glove out, and secure Davey Johnson's deep flyball to left field, Jones bent his left knee toward the ground in a genuflecting motion. Indeed, New York's far-fetched prayers were answered.

The Mets had many saviors who guided them to baseball's promised land. Among those supplying the offense, Jones proved to be the most impactful. Hitting .340, which endured as the team's highest single-season average for nearly three decades, he was a bat New York could not do without. Until David Wright's emergence, it could have been argued that Cleon was the best pure hitter the Mets produced. An inarguable point is that he became the franchise's first consistent bat.

It's quite possible Cleon was destined for success simply based on his origin. Hailing from Alabama, the same home state as Willie Mays and Hank Aaron, Jones was a baseball and football standout at both County High School in Mobile and at Alabama A&M.

Signed during the Mets' inaugural season of 1962, the team got cursory looks at Jones in 1963 and 1965, with a significant minor-league stint in between. He not only became a starter by the 1966 season, he was the leadoff hitter on Opening Day. From there, Cleon gave brief glimpses of what was to come, but not before learning some hard lessons. Jones got himself into a tailspin he couldn't get out of in 1967. Prolonged slumps, benchings, and public criticism from manager Wes Westrum: a thumbnail sketch of a forgettable year.

But transformative changes were on the horizon that would positively impact both Jones and the Mets. First, Gil Hodges was brought on as manager that November. A month later, New York acquired Tommie Agee, a fellow Mobile native and Cleon's high school friend and teammate. The trade for Agee to the Mets from the White Sox provided more than just a familiar face in the clubhouse. It moved Jones from center field, a spot with which he was never comfortable, to left field. Agee was inserted in center and would play it as well as any Met ever has.

While Agee's bat never got going in his initial National League season, Cleon came out of an early slump in June to become one of the NL's best in batting average. In a year when the scales were tipped sharply in the pitcher's favor, Jones hit .297 when only six other major leaguers could creep above .300. It was a 51-point improvement from the season before, while his on-base percentage went up by 59 points.

With the direction and faith instilled by Hodges, Jones showed that comfortable surroundings could yield better results. He took it a step further in 1969, while his team took a giant leap. Cleon started fast, hitting .410 for April, blasting five homers in May, and posting a June batting average of .341 to catapult the Mets into a position to challenge the Chicago Cubs for first place.

His hot start earned Jones a nod as an All-Star starter. He made good on that selection with two hits in four trips to the plate.

A hurt leg during the second half didn't stop Cleon in challenging the likes of Pete Rose and Roberto Clemente for the batting crown. Jones hit safely in 24 of the 29 games he played in that August. Jones ended up five points shy of Clemente and eight behind Rose, but his .340 average would go unmatched by a Met until John Olerud surpassed it 29 years later.

Jones cut his strikeouts down by 38 from 1968 and led the club in on-base percentage at .422. He was second on the team in RBIs, one short of the vastly improved Agee, and seventh in the National League Most Valuable Player voting. But Jones was by no means a one-dimensional contributor to the "Miracle Mets." His .991 fielding percentage was second among all NL outfielders and his range factor was first.

Cleon's prowess at the plate picked up steam when the playoffs began. In the opening game of the inaugural National League Championship Series, his eighth-inning RBI double keyed a five-run frame. He went 3-for-5 with a homer in Game 2 and tallied two more hits in four at-bats in Game 3. This clout was of little surprise given what he had done over the regular season, but his efforts were part of a team-wide offensive breakout. New York swept Atlanta in the best-of-five series by outscoring the Braves 27–15, belting six homers, and hitting .327.

Cleon Jones was the best homegrown hitter the Mets produced during their first two decades. Jones hit .340 for the "Miracle Mets."

In the World Series victory, Jones hit only .158, but certainly made his presence known. As he led off the bottom of the sixth with the Mets behind 3–0 in Game 5, his claim that a Dave McNally pitch hit him in the foot was supported by Hodges, who showed the home plate umpire a smudge of shoe polish on the ball. This initiated the Mets rally that finished off the Orioles and cemented the Mets as champions.

The 1969 season was undoubtably Jones's best for many reasons, but his best two weeks came during the pennant chase of 1973 as he salvaged what was nearly a lost year.

Jones, like much of the Mets roster, couldn't escape an onslaught of injuries threatening to keep New York out of NL East title contention. Heading into September, Cleon's bum leg had reduced him to 70 games. His bat and body were almost completely void of power with only five home runs (two of which came on Opening Day) and 12 doubles. Despite the bothersome knee, Jones rediscovered his potent swing. He batted .278 after September 19, but belted six home runs and 14 RBIs and led the charge as the Mets emerged from a crowded six-team scramble with the division crown.

New York didn't as much win the East as they survived it. The Mets showed they were the best team—and the luckiest. Never was there a better example than on September 20, when Jones took part in a play that indicated there was still some magic left over from 1969.

With two outs and Richie Zisk on first in the top of the 13th against then-first-place Pittsburgh, Dave Augustine sent one beyond Jones's reach in left field—ticketed to land in the Mets bullpen. But this ball had Mets destiny written all over it. The trajectory bounced it squarely off the top of the fence and back toward Jones. An inch farther, it's a home run. An inch shorter, it's an awkward ricochet. In either instance, a run scores.

Jones caught it from the fortuitous rebound, turned, and fired to cutoff man Wayne Garrett while Zisk rounded third and headed home. Garrett threw to catcher Ron Hodges, who laid down the tag on a sliding Zisk.

"We were very fortunate to be able to make a play on that," he said. "That was the turning point in the Mets winning the championship."

Jones's contributions to the Mets as they journeyed again through the NLCS and up to the seventh game of the World Series were timely if not nearly as significant.

His power subsided, but his Game 2 ninth-inning RBI single made way for three additional runs and provided the necessary cushion in Jon Matlack's dazzling performance. A wall-banging double in the bottom of the fifth in Game 5 broke a 2–2 tie in what would become a 7–2 pennant-clinching victory. Clutch hits were harder to come by in the seven-game World Series defeat to Oakland. Cleon went 8-for-28 with three extra-base hits and a Game 2 homer.

The injuries that nearly sent his '73 season up in smoke were a theme for the second half of his career. Jones went relatively unscathed in the post-championship seasons. In 1970, his average dropped more than 60 points but he remained second in the club in hits and doubles. The Mets toyed with first place into mid-September before finishing third. Cleon reclaimed his spot as an elite National League hitter in 1971, a year in which the Mets were grasping for offense. In addition to batting .319, he paced New York in hits and RBIs, and his 14 home runs— while not a staggering total—were good enough to tie for the team lead.

But 1972 is when his aches and pains got the better of him, and his team unwelcomingly joined in. Without much depth behind Jones, newcomer Rusty Staub, and several others, the Mets were unable to absorb losses of that significance. Cleon limped through 106 games and batted just .245—his lowest since '67—with five homers and 12 doubles.

Jones had a slight revival in 1974 despite continued knee aggravation. He managed to eclipse 60 RBIs and 20 doubles for the first time in three years. Jones underwent off-season surgery with the hopes of getting fully healthy, but his career would soon end unceremoniously.

Cleon's Mets tenure didn't transpire without controversy or, at least, perceived controversy. Nursing a sore leg, Jones casually fielded a base hit on a soggy day in late July 1969, which prompted Gil Hodges to come out to left field and remove his .346 hitter and All-Star in the middle of an inning. Jones has since downplayed the episode as Hodges simply taking out a valuable player who was clearly hobbling. But it served as a wake-up call for the team and has become an anecdotal subplot that perhaps sparked the weeks and months that followed.

The incident in May 1975 marked his permanent discharge, regardless of any equity he had previously built in a Mets uniform.

The operation to repair Jones's knee after the '74 season forced him into an extended spring training in Florida. There, he engaged in and was charged with indecent exposure after being found by police in a van with a woman who was not his wife. The charges were dropped, but that didn't stop team chairman M. Donald Grant from fining Cleon $2,000 and making him publicly apologize next to his wife.

The shaming tactics didn't stop. Grant insisted Jones get less playing time when he came back to action. Perturbed by his new role as a benchwarmer, Cleon refused manager Yogi Berra's call for him to take left field for late-inning defense. Following the incident, Jones, whose leverage had been repressed by a depreciating body and diminished skills, was given his release.

It was an abrupt end for someone who, upon his exit, had more hits, more home runs, and more RBIs than any other Met while playing a significant part in two pennant-winning teams and a world championship. It's clear that no offensive player in the first dozen years of this franchise was more impactful.

RESERVE LEFT FIELDER—MICHAEL CONFORTO

Peruse the deep recesses of Mets conversation on Twitter, and you're bound to find every kind of thought on just about every player. Mention of Conforto has elicited a host of differing opinions: "overrated," "cornerstone," "streaky," "underrated."

If you think he would be affected by what others have said on social media, he's faced assorted doubts before. Minor league scouts praised his fluid line drive swing with power to all fields while lamenting his defensive liabilities, and even the Mets might have had their questions when his early progression looked more like an elevation chart than a straight line.

But recent success and the totality of his five seasons indicate the impressive company Conforto already keeps. By the time 2019 concluded, a year marked by a personal-high 33 home runs, Conforto had accumulated 109 for his career—which moved him into 12th on the franchise's all-time list. He also joined exclusive Mets company that same year, as he became one of five to tally hit at least 25 homers in four consecutive seasons.

Signs of his potential were evident at Oregon State, and his polished offensive credentials had the Mets eager to select him with the 10th choice in the 2014 draft. Those same talents allowed him to accelerate through the minor league system within 13 months.

He debuted on July 24, 2015, as the 1,000th player to wear a Mets uniform, and after an 0-for-4 night, registered four hits in five at-bats the next evening. As the calendar turned, Conforto made sure his indoctrination into the majors wouldn't impede New York's playoff push.

He registered his first homer on August 3, the same night the Mets moved into first place—a position they held for the remainder of the season. In 56 games, Conforto batted .270 with 14 doubles, nine home runs, 30 runs scored, and 26 RBIs. His .841 OPS was second on the team behind only Yoenis Céspedes, and despite playing in fewer than half his team's games, his 2.1 WAR (according to Fangraphs) ranked sixth.

But the most unexpected revelation was the defensive skills that were far more adequate than the scouting reports indicated. Conforto not only displayed a strong and accurate throwing arm from left field, but he also showed off some surprising range and excellent instincts for a player of his age and experience. He finished his abbreviated year with six outfield assists, a 7.5 UZR, and nine defensive runs saved—the second-best total on the team.

Conforto's terrific first impression allowed him to hang on during the Mets' journey through the postseason. Even after struggling through the NLDS and NLCS, he wasn't fazed by the World Series stage. In Game 4 against the Kansas City

When Michael Conforto hit his 100th career home run on August 7, 2019, he became the second-fastest in Mets history to reach the century mark.

MATT ROURKE/AP/SHUTTERSTOCK

Royals, Conforto blasted two home runs—becoming the first rookie to do so since Andruw Jones in 1996 and the first Met to do it since Gary Carter in '86. Following a third-inning homer pulled into the right-field upper deck, he sent a rocket over the right-field wall to lead off the fifth.

"He's dangerous, and tonight he showed that," said manager Terry Collins. "This guy is going to be an outstanding offensive player."

If 2015 was predominately a joyride, 2016 was a seesaw.

Conforto lived up to the high praise he was receiving from those within the organization, as he shot out of the gate to begin—what he hoped—was his first full year in the majors. From Opening Day through April 30, the Mets' new starting left fielder looked like a permanent fixture and a star-in-waiting when he recorded 10 multi-hit games, batted .365, had an on-base percentage of .442, and an OPS of 1.118.

Then came the harsh brush with reality that some newcomers endure. Conforto probably felt it harder than most. Looking so confident in the first month, he totally fell off the table during a seven-week period in which he hit .130. Conforto was in need of a substantial adjustment, and that kind of fix would have to come in Triple-A, the step he skipped on his quick ascension through the minors the previous year. Conforto racked up plenty of frequent flier miles as he served multiple stints in Las Vegas.

"It was tough, especially not having really experienced that scale of struggle before," he said.

The shuttle from the desert to the Big Apple didn't show its effects right away. For 2016, the end result was a paltry .220 batting average along with 12 home runs, 42 RBIs and a glaringly bad 89 strikeouts in 304 at-bats.

Conforto had to earn his way into the starting lineup in 2017—and he did. Then he became an All-Star, with a .285 average and a .403 on-base percentage through the first half, and seemed back on his original trajectory.

In a year swirling with misfortune, Conforto was the lone Mets hitter who remained a bastion of stability and promise. Then came August 24. On a routine swing-and-miss, Conforto collapsed to the dirt in agony. Perfectly capturing 2017's theme, he dislocated his left shoulder and tore his posterior capsule—adding to the heap of injuries that had piled up over the course of an incredible season. Conforto's impressive year ended abruptly at 27 home runs and 68 RBIs, while his .939 OPS and 146 wRC+ were in the top 20 among MLB hitters.

But he faced an uncertain future as to whether or not the harm to his vital joint would curtail his ascendance. After a poor start to 2018 (in which he batted just .216 at midseason), he was fully recovered by year's end. Conforto exploded in the second half with a 143 wRC+, and his stats elsewhere surged too. His final month was especially encouraging; he blasted nine homers and posted a 165 wRC+ over his last 112 plate appearances. When the final totals were tallied, Michael's home runs (28), RBIs (82), and runs scored (78) quelled any fears that the injury from last year would have a lingering effect.

Now the hope was that he could regain his 2017 level of performance for an entire year. Luckily for Conforto, the focus of the 2019 offense wasn't squarely centered on him. The conditions were ideal for the 26-year-old to blossom. Joined by rookie home run sensation Pete Alonso, .300-plus batting wizard Jeff McNeil, versatile Amed Rosario, and surprising newcomer J. D. Davis, Conforto benefited from a vastly improved lineup that fashioned the most prolific power season in Mets history.

After a ragged start, New York embarked on a thrilling stretch shortly after the All-Star break, highlighted by 15 wins in 16 games, which vaulted the Mets into wild card contention. Conforto was a crucial element behind their newfound success—socking seven homers and driving in 15 runs during that span.

On August 9, before a Citi Field atmosphere reminiscent of games played during Conforto's rookie year, the Mets erased a three-run ninth-inning deficit to the Washington Nationals on Todd Frazier's left-field pole–wrapping home run. Shortly after, Conforto pulled a tracer over the head of right fielder Adam Eaton to score Juan Lagares with the winning score. His first career walk-off hit capped a victory as thrilling as any in recent memory, made more memorable by the on-field jubilation that followed. The Mets swarmed Conforto, with Alonso ripping off his jersey in celebration. The Polar Bear attack left Michael a bare-chested hero.

Although the Mets ran out of steam in their chase for a playoff spot, Conforto further validated his case as an essential piece of the team's future while verifying his place relative to other power hitters through the years. He became just the fifth player in Mets history to record at least 30 homers, 80 walks, and 90 RBIs—joining David Wright, Darryl Strawberry, Carlos Beltrán, and Howard Johnson. It was also the fourth time in five years he finished with an OPS+ of better than 120.

"I'm lucky to play in New York," he said. "Sometimes I take it on the chin. But when you're going well, damn, it's great."

Starting Center Fielder—Carlos Beltrán

Eight hundred seventy-eight of his swings for the orange and blue resulted in hits and 149 ended as home runs. But it's the swing he didn't make—on a knee-bending Adam Wainwright curveball to end the 2006 NLCS and a Mets season seemingly destined for the World Series—that remains the lasting memory.

The context of when it took place makes it the moment we most associate with Beltrán. To use it as a defining moment is an oversimplification. A wide-lens view of his Mets career proves—despite the grand expectations laid upon him from the start—that while he was understated, he wasn't an underachiever.

Beltrán averaged 30 homers, 108 RBIs, and 39 doubles per 162 games over his six full seasons with nary a fist pump or a bat flip. He also etched his name into franchise history in 2006 when he equaled the Mets' then-single-season home run mark, a record that had stood for 13 years, while also driving in a career-high 116 runs. And before surgery wreaked havoc on his knee, he was among the most successful and timely baserunners, stealing around 20 a year at an 84 percent clip.

But the most downplayed aspect of his well-rounded talents was his defense. Beltrán's range made him an elite center fielder and a three-time Gold Glove recipient. He got to would-be hits gracefully, not acrobatically. His speed and his knack for reading the ball off opposing hitters' bats afforded him the ability to glide over to catches more often than sliding. Grass stains were rarely visible on his uniform. Beltrán's smooth approach made him impervious to the spectacular play—a rare exception being the remarkable 2005 catch that scaled the now defunct center-field hill at Houston's Minute Maid Park.

The blend of his broad, quiet skills with his ordinary demeanor and an absence of verbosity made him ripe for criticism, especially when the Mets were unable to return to the postseason (often despite him, not because of him).

Even so, Beltrán often served as a target of fans and media, especially as the Mets' window of opportunity for reaching the World Series began to shrink. Unsubstantiated claims ranged from his unwillingness to play through injuries and, when he was healthy, not giving his full effort.

"The way they think of me, that's how they feel, so there's nothing I can do about it," he said soon after being traded in 2011. "I just have to say that, in my time here, I really enjoyed playing for the Mets. We went through a lot of ups and downs as a team, but I feel, personally, that in the years that I was healthy, I did the best that I could to help the team."

But Beltrán never catered to public demands nor did he appeal to its desires. According to a 2009 *New York* magazine article, "Many of Beltrán's best talents are subtle, and subtlety doesn't always win you friends in baseball. . . . Subtlety might be even less appreciated in New York."

How he was courted to Queens was anything but modest. The 1999 American League Rookie of the Year parlayed an astounding 2004 postseason performance with Houston into a free-agency bidding war.

New general manager Omar Minaya, like several other team executives, was rightly enamored of the mastery he demonstrated on the October stage, including eight homers, 20 hits, a .435 batting average, and an on-base percentage above .500. All this came following a stellar regular season that saw him eclipse 30 home runs for the first time in his still young career and surpass the 100-RBI barrier for the fifth time in his six years.

Who was to fault the Mets for salivating over the prospect of a 27-year-old switch-hitting, five-tool center fielder teamed with a pair of up-and-coming infielders named Wright and Reyes along with fellow free-agency pickup Pedro Martínez?

During his seven-year stay in Queens, Carlos Beltrán won three Gold Gloves and made five All-Star teams. His 31.1 WAR is third-highest among all Mets position players.
KEITH ALLISON/WIKIMEDIA COMMONS

For fans who had suffered through a third straight miserable season, no price—not even $119 million over seven years—was too much, even if they weren't the ones spending it.

Beltrán became a very rich man, but also a marked man. It would be hard to live up to his lucrative new deal. And in year one, it was hard—but not solely because of his own failings.

Beltrán suffered career lows in batting average (.266), home runs (16), RBIs (78), runs scored (83), and stolen bases (17), which planted the seeds for scrutiny. He could never get situated in his first season in Queens. Much of that was due to nagging quadriceps, but a more gruesome injury, on August 11 in San Diego, set him back further. A diving head-to-head collision with Mike Cameron, going after a ball in shallow right-center field, left Beltrán with vertigo. (Cameron suffered a concussion, a temporary loss of vision, and broken cheekbones.)

Physically rehabilitated and more comfortable in his surroundings, Beltrán rebounded in 2006 with arguably the best season of his two-decade major-league career and perhaps the most well-rounded offensive season any Met has ever assembled.

He set one Mets record—127 runs scored—and tied two others—80 extra-base hits and 41 home runs. None of those homers was more notable than the blow he struck—against the Cardinals, interestingly enough—which capped off a thrilling Mets comeback on August 22. St. Louis likely thought it was safely ahead with a 7–1 lead in the fifth and a 7–6 lead in the ninth. In both instances, they thought wrong. Beltrán's two-run walk-off homer only added to the assurance that the Mets were the best in the National League. Of course, they came up one win short of proving it.

Cliched or not, the Mets probably wouldn't have reached that point without Beltrán's presence in the lineup or his fluidity in patrolling center field. He finished fourth in NL MVP voting but was clearly the most valuable Met. Beltrán's 8.2 WAR was easily the highest on the team and far better than the next best, José Reyes (5.9). He even delivered three home runs in that fateful NLCS versus St. Louis, but it soon was forgotten.

While the outcome of the series was needlessly placed on Beltrán for taking a called third strike on the Adam Wainwright curve, the pitch was—according to FanGraphs—one of the most effective in recent memory and one that has fooled many great hitters. It would have been a bit less frustrating had he swung and missed, but no less painful.

What hurt even more in the subsequent seasons is that the Mets never returned to the postseason during the Beltrán era. It wasn't just that they missed out, it was how it happened.

New York unraveled to relinquish would-be playoff spots in 2007 and 2008. Beltrán, though, was one of the few Mets who never caved under the late-season pressure. Poor managerial decisions, dreadful bullpens, and the lackluster performances of his teammates were most to blame for their eleventh-hour failings. Beltrán tried to right a sinking ship in September '07 by launching eight homers and driving in 27 runs (more than he had in any other month that year). In September 2008, he hit .344 with an on-base percentage of .440 and an OPS of 1.086.

Through 596 games as a Met, Beltrán continued to live up to his five-tool profile: 117 home runs, 418 RBIs, 145 doubles, 83 stolen bases, a pair of Silver Slugger awards, three Gold Gloves, and three All-Star Games. But any chance to stay on the field regularly in 2009 was ruined by an injury that accentuated a bizarre year—even by Mets standards. It's unclear if Citi Field had a hex put on it before the ribbon was cut, but seemingly nobody—Beltrán in particular—was immune to the voodoo.

He went through a revolving door of diagnoses, bad medical advice, and physical setbacks over an ailing right knee that put him out of action for 10 weeks. Although he managed to hit .325, Beltrán's partial season of adequate-to-full health limited him to 10 homers and 48 RBIs.

The interminable quest to return to 100 percent did not end. Beltrán even underwent surgery in January 2010 without team permission. It was July 15 when he officially came back on a major-league diamond. And the absence proved too long a delay to salvage his old form.

The surgically repaired knee slowed Beltrán considerably. He had swiped 83 bases in the two seasons before he signed with New York. In the seven seasons after, he stole 100. But he was almost never caught, a reminder of the baseball intelligence he brought to the Mets.

Entering the final year of his contract in 2011, Beltrán made a concerted effort to return to his previous standards and silence the doubters.

"I wanted to prove to people that doubt me that they were wrong," he said, "that I was going to be able to play at the high level that I know I can play."

A rejuvenated and incentivized Beltrán reached All-Star level with 30 doubles and 15 homers through a little more than half a season. He became the eighth Met to hit three home runs in a game on May 12. Most importantly, he stayed healthy.

But with New York out of contention and free agency looming for their center fielder at year's end, it made sense to shop him around at the trade deadline. The Giants bought, sending prized pitching prospect Zack Wheeler east. The Mets strengthened their farm system but parted with a clubhouse leader.

"He's the guy that always took me out, talked to me all the time," José Reyes said. "When things weren't going good for me, he'd come to my locker and talk to me for a little while. And I appreciated that."

Beltrán's relatively insignificant shortcomings, propelled mostly by suboptimal health, were magnified because he was an immense talent who was never coated in entertainment value and, perhaps, because he was never tied to one team—wearing the uniforms of seven different clubs during his 20 years.

With no other franchise did he play longer (seven years), produce more homers (149), drive in more runs (559), hit more doubles (208), or score more runs (551) than the Mets. And those numbers would have been bolstered if not for his injuries. Of his nine All-Star selections, five came while he played in Queens. Considering how his totals warrant Hall of Fame inclusion, and despite the events that led to his quick dismissal as manager, it's not a stretch to think he could one day be representing the Mets in Cooperstown.

Beltrán's prolific career in New York doesn't deserve to be fixated on a strikeout or anything that happened afterwards. It deserves much more respect. And by placing him in the starting lineup of this all-time team, he gets that respect here.

FIRST RESERVE CENTER FIELDER—MOOKIE WILSON

The "little roller up along first," which went between the legs of Bill Buckner during the climax of Game 6 of the 1986 World Series, was not solely a product of good fortune. Two of Mookie's superlatives—his steadfast resolve and breakneck speed—made the culmination of the franchise's iconic comeback complete.

Wilson prolonged his two-out at-bat against Bob Stanley, fighting off pitches and working the count, before the Red Sox reliever uncorked a wild pitch that allowed Kevin

Mitchell to score from third base and tie the score. And when he ultimately put the ball in play, the quickness that made him the team's stolen base leader might have allowed him to beat Buckner to first base anyway, even if the grounder was fielded cleanly.

While a summation of his Mets career can be boiled down to a five-minute, season-on-the-line scenario, Mookie's immense popularity spawned from all-out effort, regardless of circumstances, while never deviating from his optimistic outlook and constant enthusiasm.

Such an endearing quality was evident in the mid-to-late 1980s—when the Mets were fighting for division titles, pennants, and world championships—and equally apparent in the early part of the decade, when the Mets were merely fighting for respectability.

Mookie knew no other way than hustle and hard work. It was an attitude born of hot, sultry days working the fields in tiny Bamburg, South Carolina, in a family with barely enough funds to scrape by. Baseball was an escape from the hard labor and, eventually, from poverty.

A second-round draft selection by the Mets in 1977, Wilson shone for the University of South Carolina as he led the Gamecocks to a College World Series appearance. USC fell short, but Mookie got a ring with the Double-A Jackson Mets—a wedding ring. On June 22, 1978, Wilson married Rosa Gilbert in a ceremony conducted at home plate at Smith-Wills Stadium. "My wife wanted a big diamond," he said.

By August 1980, after racking up 99 steals in two seasons at Triple-A, the Mets brought Mookie to the bigs as a small step in their steep rebuilding plan. For a franchise languishing in desolation, Wilson offered a jolt of energy. He also presented something the Mets hadn't had before: a homegrown position player who could steal bases with impunity. The strike-shortened 1981 season showed that was possible. His 24 steals were eighth in the NL.

But while stealing bases wasn't a problem for Wilson, getting on base was. His inability to draw walks belied the requisite skill for a leadoff man and served as cause for managerial reluctance to slot him at the top of the order. His on-base percentage went from a meager .317 in 1981 to a .314 in 1982 and dropped to a glaringly low .300 in 1983. It didn't help that his strikeout totals eclipsed the century mark twice. But his speed proved an overwhelming factor. During that same three-year span, Mookie batted first in all but 14 games he started and stole 136 bases.

Under new manager Davey Johnson in 1984, he ceded leadoff responsibilities primarily to Wally Backman. Although Wilson played in more games, he naturally had fewer at-bats. He tallied fewer hits, too, but produced more doubles (28), more triples (10), and more homers (10) than in any other season before or since. Mookie also ranked as the second-best center fielder in the league in terms of fielding percentage.

While his range was more than adequate, his arm was mediocre—and it didn't improve when he began experiencing discomfort in his shoulder for the first half of 1985. By July, it was too painful to continue. On pace to top his '84 totals, Mookie underwent surgery that sidelined him for almost two months and kept him from improving on eight triples and 24 stolen bases.

All the anticipation that surrounded 1986 was of little importance to Wilson after what happened in spring training. During a rundown drill, he was struck in the eye by an

In direct contrast to the outlaws who populated the 1986 club, Mookie Wilson charmed fans with his hustle and thousand-watt smile.

inadvertent throw—shattering his glasses. Mookie took 21 stitches above the eye and four more on the side of his nose and was out until early May.

But his old job wasn't waiting for him when he returned. Anybody who subscribes to the myth that injuries can't lose you a starting spot wasn't privy to the Wilson–Lenny Dykstra conundrum. Mookie found himself sharing center field duties with Dykstra, a pint-sized ball of energy who developed into a catalyst for the '86 team in his first full season.

Contrary to how most would feel, Wilson begrudgingly swallowed his pride and accepted his fate while praising the emerging youngster. It was not until George Foster was released in early August that Wilson settled back into the starting lineup and got more consistent turns at the plate. A re-energized Mookie batted .330 in August with a .400 on-base percentage, nine extra-base hits, and 17 RBIs. His average for the season went as high as .302 in mid-September before a late slump pushed it down to .289.

Those struggles carried into the playoffs. But a 3-for-26 NLCS became an afterthought by the sixth game when he and his center field cohort combined to ignite the most important rally to date. After Dykstra led off with a triple, Mookie followed by sending an 0-2 Bob Knepper pitch barely over the outstretched reach of second baseman Bill Doran. That cut the Astro lead to 3–1. Wilson would come around on a Keith Hernandez double. The Mets would tie it in the ninth and win it in the 16th to advance to the Fall Classic.

And classic is the idyllic way to describe the events of October 25—along with the at-bat that is forever fixed in Mets fans' memories. With two outs, runners on first and third, and the Mets down by one, the fate of the series and the season rested in Mookie's hands. Batting from the left side and facing Bob Stanley, Wilson held the responsibility of staving off the daunting potential of elimination. Any swing could have been the last.

He fouled off four of six pitches, working the count to 2-2, before Stanley let one loose. The pitch scooted past Mookie's flailing legs and catcher Rich Gedman's glove. As it went to the backstop, Kevin Mitchell raced in from third base. Ray Knight advanced into scoring position.

That was an incredible occurrence, but it would pale against what happened next.

With pressure lessened, Mookie continued to swing freely, spoiling two more pitches. Finally, he hit a fair grounder slowly toward first base, a grounder fitted with destiny's eyes.

Past the glove and through the legs of Bill Buckner it went. An astonished Knight rounded third and touched home amid a swarm of teammates while Shea was sent into its most exultant state.

Mookie would play a part in the Game 7 victory, too. He singled and scored in a three-run sixth-inning rally that brought New York even.

In defending their championship, the Mets made no effort to clear the outfield logjam. Versatile Kevin Mitchell went to San Diego, but coming in return was Kevin McReynolds—the soon-to-be starting left fielder.

The acquisition did not sit well with Wilson or Dykstra. The usually congenial Mookie went so far as to request a trade, which was ignored. Frustrated and motivated, Wilson earned his best batting average (.299), on-base percentage (.359), and OPS (.814). Although he wasn't stealing bases as frequently, Mookie managed 19 doubles and seven triples in 385 at-bats.

Wilson and Dykstra continued to take turns in center field in 1988, but an early Mookie slump—despite the Mets maintaining a safe lead in the NL East standings—suggested he was on the decline. Through July, having participated in 65 games and started 48, he was hitting .236 with 19 RBIs and 31 runs scored. But Wilson turned things around in August. He had 29 hits for the month—more than he recorded in the previous two months combined—elevating his batting average by 41 points. His hot bat sizzled through the end of the regular season as he garnered more playing time. From August 6 on, he hit .386, drove in 21 runs, and scored 30 more. Mookie brought his strikeout-to-walk ratio to a respectable 63-27 and even showed some power—belting five home runs. But Wilson's triumphs were muffled as the Mets ventured into a playoff meeting with Los Angeles. His tie-breaking hit in the eighth inning of Game 3 would be his lone impact. A 2-for-13 showing and an injured thumb made the choice for Davey Johnson to use Dykstra in each of the three remaining games an easy one.

The Mets showed faith in Wilson when they picked up his option before the 1989 season. But while a trade of Dykstra seemed to signal Wilson's permanence, the exchange with Philadelphia brought over Juan Samuel, who the Mets tried to convert into an outfielder. Wilson again requested his exit. This time, the Mets answered his plea, sending him to Toronto just before the trade deadline.

José Reyes has since overtaken Wilson's stolen bases and triples records, but he'll never surpass Mookie's popularity. Not many can. Statistics don't paint the full picture of his legacy, as evidenced by sustained admiration for him beyond producing the franchise's most memorable at-bat. To many

Mets fans, he's forever number one in their program and number one in their hearts.

SECOND RESERVE CENTER FIELDER—TOMMIE AGEE

The debate over who made the greatest catch in World Series history could go on forever. But the debate over who made the *two* greatest catches in the annals of the Fall Classic begins and ends with Agee in 1969.

His supernatural glove work was the showstopper—and run stopper—in Game 3. With two out and two on in the top of the fourth, the Orioles' Elrod Hendricks had what appeared to be an extra base hit in the gap. Agee raced to his right, turned the mitt on his left hand as he neared the "396" mark in left-center field, and made a backhanded snag just before coming into contact with the fence.

Then came the encore—in the seventh inning with bases loaded and Paul Blair at the plate. Blair sent an 0-2 pitch from Nolan Ryan to right-center. Agee sped over and made a sliding catch as he dove on the warning track.

This pair of defensive plays embedded in World Series lore collectively prevented at least five potential Baltimore runs in what would become a 5–0 Mets victory and a 2-1 series edge for New York.

And you wouldn't guess who kicked off the scoring. Or maybe you would. It was simply Agee's day—both in stopping the Orioles and igniting the Mets. He led off the bottom of the first inning against Jim Palmer with a hit no defender could catch.

While his Game 3 homer carried the most importance, a home run earlier in the year was his most impressive. It came on April 20. A sparse crowd of barely over 8,000 witnessed the only fair ball to reach the left-field upper deck stands at Shea Stadium.

Agee would go on to lead the eventual world champs in home runs with 26, runs scored with 97, and RBIs with 76. Getting there, though, required a healthy dose of perseverance from the Mobile, Alabama, native and a great deal of patience from a manager who believed in his abilities.

In 1966, Agee caught the eye of the American League, including Gil Hodges (then leading the Washington Senators), when he slugged 22 homers and stole 44 bases on his way to winning Rookie of the Year for the Chicago White Sox. But as he struggled during his sophomore season, Agee—who often let slumps get into his head—wasn't helped by the public criticisms from manager Eddie Stanky.

Hodges understood that a different approach could rekindle the talents within Agee while rectifying one of the franchise's glaring problem areas. So when Gil was hired to take over the Mets, he knew the young outfielder could fulfill many of their needs.

"The first thing Hodges wanted to do when he became the manager was to acquire Tommie Agee," the late general manager Johnny Murphy said. "He wanted a guy to bat leadoff with speed [who] could hit for power. He also . . . needed a guy in center to run the ball down."

On December 15, 1967, New York traded for the 25-year-old along with utility player Al Weis, who would eventually share in 1969 World Series heroism.

Agee's hopes of a smooth National League transition got a rude awakening by that period's lord of intimidation, Bob Gibson. In his first spring training at-bat, the Cardinals right-hander—renowned for enacting this sort of welcome—beaned him with a high fastball.

Tommie Agee saved many runs with his center-field defense, but his glove was never more valuable than in Game 3 of the 1969 World Series.
NATIONAL BASEBALL HALL OF FAME

It set the tone for a rough and disjointed season. A brutal 0-for-34 funk in April sank his confidence, and he struggled to regain it. Agee didn't register a homer or an RBI until May 10. He ended the year with just five home runs, 17 runs driven in, and a .217 batting average in 391 at-bats. Yet Agee thrived in patrolling center field with his usual aplomb—not an easy chore amid the swirling winds that engulfed Shea's atmosphere.

"I hated it; every guy before me hated it," recalled fellow Mobile native and longtime friend Cleon Jones, who played center in the two years prior to Agee's arrival. "But Tommie never complained. I watched Willie Mays, Curt Flood, Vada Pinson—a lot of guys came into this Shea Stadium outfield. Nobody played it better than Tommie Agee."

But for the Mets to succeed, much less contend for the pennant, in 1969, his production at the plate had to improve. Hodges was fully aware of this.

As Wayne Coffey wrote in his 2019 book, *They Said It Couldn't Be Done*: "All through the spring, and beyond, Hodges probably had Agee in his office more than any other player. An uncanny reader of his players' psyches, Hodges knew Agee was embarrassed by his performance and was prone to over-thinking and getting in his own way when he was slumping. Again and again, Hodges told Agee that he was his center-fielder, and nothing would change that. The manager never wavered."

After slugging two homers in the third game of the year, including the prodigious upper-deck shot at Shea, Agee went into a deep tailspin: 3-for-29. That prompted Gil to take a somewhat drastic measure to ensure there wouldn't be a repeat of 1968.

The Mets skipper gave his struggling center fielder what now would be called a mental health break. Not just a day off—but ten. Agee got the chance to press the reset button and eventually began swinging like he was accustomed to. He burst out of his malaise by batting .311 in May and ultimately became National League Comeback Player of the Year.

Agee's personal awakening coincided handsomely with the Mets' rise to prominence.

The Chicago Cubs' lead over New York went from 10 games on August 13 to a scant 2.5 by the time they engaged in a crucial pair of contests at Shea Stadium.

An innocent bystander during a beanball tussle between Bill Hands, Tom Seaver, and Ron Santo in a May series, Agee suddenly found himself square in the middle of a brushback war. Hands started the opener for Chicago and rekindled the firestorm with a pitch that whizzed perilously close to Agee's head.

Koosman stood up for his teammate by plunking Ron Santo to start the top of the second, but Agee had a more effective retaliatory measure. Undeterred by the chin music and picking up the slack for an injured Cleon Jones, he took Hands deep with a runner on base. The Cubs evened the score in the top of the sixth, but the Mets answered back in the bottom half as Agee doubled and scored on a Wayne Garrett single. When Agee slid and touched the plate ahead of catcher Randy Hundley's tag, the Chicago backstop leaped and pleaded his displeasure like a child who'd been denied his ice cream.

New York carried the momentum from that 3–2 victory into a win the next night behind Tom Seaver and again the following evening versus Montreal, which put the Mets atop the standings for the first time ever and for the rest of 1969.

Agee's postseason success wasn't limited to Game 3 of the World Series. He shook off an 0-for-5 in the opener of the NLCS with Atlanta to reach base in seven of his 11 plate appearances made over the final two games of a Mets sweep—including a pair of homers and four RBIs.

The reputation Agee cultivated through his sorcery with the leather against the Baltimore Orioles carried over through the 1970 season as he captured his second Gold Glove Award—a career-high 13 errors notwithstanding.

Agee also improved in several offensive categories relative to his '69 output by raising his batting average by 15 points (.286), upping his doubles total by seven (30), and stealing 19 more bases (31). He set multiple team records, including runs scored and total bases (both bested by Darryl Strawberry in 1987). Agee assembled hit streaks of 20 and 19 games and hit for the cycle on July 6. This occurred soon after a red-hot June that saw him belt 11 round-trippers and drive in 32 runs while batting .364. The 24 homers he totaled made him the first Met to eclipse 20 in multiple seasons and the first to lead the team in that category twice.

Any chance of staying atop the Mets leaderboard for the next two years was thwarted by a rash of injuries—specifically knee problems. It began in August 1970, when he suffered cartilage damage sliding into home. Agee dealt with this hindrance for the better part of two years and it showed. His 1972 batting average tumbled to a woeful .227, accompanied by a paltry 47 RBIs.

His physical deterioration was the main reason his career was done at 30. Retirement came much too early. Sadly, so did the end of his life. On January 22, 2001, at 58, Agee collapsed and died of a heart attack.

Before his passing, Agee had been, among other things, a restaurant owner and mortgage insurance salesman—ordinary jobs for a man who performed extraordinary feats in baseball's greatest showcase with a pair of plays in the World Series highlight reel that will live on forever.

The New York Mets All-Time All-Star Team Starting Lineup		
1	José Reyes	SS
2	David Wright	3B
3	Keith Hernandez	1B
4	Mike Piazza	C
5	Darryl Strawberry	RF
6	Carlos Beltrán	CF
7	Cleon Jones	LF
8	Edgardo Alfonzo	2B
9	Tom Seaver	P

8

MANAGER

GIL HODGES

In the story of any franchise, there are a few shining, seminal moments. The insertion of Hodges as manager is certainly one of them. There were a lot of reasons the Mets were crowned champions in 1969—brilliant pitching from Tom Seaver, Jerry Koosman's outstanding defense, and timely hitting. But none of that would have been possible without Hodges's unwavering leadership. And that, in short, is his Mets legacy.

The influence he had on his players' careers and lives cannot be measured. Those led by Hodges don't just speak about the respect they have for him. They speak about him reverentially. The esteem in which they hold Hodges nearly 50 years after his death and more than a half-century after his most significant accomplishment is deference rarely bestowed upon any manager.

Hodges proved to be more patient than most disciplined leaders and less vocal, too. But there was never any doubting whose word was law in the Mets clubhouse. Many leaders are either feared or loved. Gil was both. No player was immune from his authority. And no player would dare question it.

As New York's field general, Hodges shed the perennial loser persona that had echoed loudly since 1962, when Gil himself was an original Met, concluding a successful career that began as a beloved Brooklyn Dodger during the 1940s and 1950s.

Hodges's tenure as an active player, during which he had accumulated more home runs than any other right-handed batter in National League history, ended when the Washington Senators asked him to lead the two-year-old club.

Under Hodges's watch, the expansion Senators gradually progressed each season, peaking at a 76-85 record and a sixth-place finish in 1967. Hodges was on the verge of a major breakthrough, but it wouldn't be with Washington.

When Wes Westrum resigned as Mets manager in September 1967, the team sought out Hodges as his replacement. From there, the Mets' fortunes changed.

His influence was felt instantaneously. Inheriting a club that had suffered 100 or more defeats in five of its first six seasons, Hodges inspired a belief that future Mets teams would be different from their predecessors.

"Gil seemed to come in with a set plan and some enthusiasm about what we could do to win," Bud Harrelson said. "I think that was conveyed to the players. We took on his confidence in us."

Gil became known for maximizing the talent at his disposal—teaching, coaching, and adjusting a lineup to ensure the greatest chance of victory. But in '68, when gauging the mental toughness of his new players, he allowed his still inexperienced team to work through tough situations and out of any rough stretches.

By year's end, the Mets had made significant headway toward respectability, even if it didn't appear that way in the

It's impossible to think the 1969 Mets would have won the World Series without Gil Hodges as their leader.

standings. New York improved by 12 games with a franchise-best 73 wins and a ninth-place finish—just the second time the Mets had reached such a height. But it was nothing compared to what took place the next year.

Anybody who contends that the Mets' world championship in 1969 was the result of a divine intervention significantly discounts the development of the team's talent and dismisses Hodges's impeccable judgment and wisdom. He utilized a platoon system more frequently, which could maximize run production for pitchers like Seaver and Koosman, who didn't need a whole lot of it to win. But for Hodges's platoon system to work, he needed to get the right players.

Gil and general manager Johnny Murphy did just that as the June 15 trade deadline neared, getting power-hitting first baseman Donn Clendenon from the newly formed Montreal Expos. The deal was an instant success. Clendenon, rejuvenated after contemplating retirement months before, was the catalyst the Mets offense was desperately seeking.

By July, the Mets had trekked into uncharted territory. They were in second place and eight games above .500, but eight games behind the Chicago Cubs—a curse-addled franchise loaded with talent but still burdened by fate.

The Mets were defying the 100–1 odds placed on them to win it all at the start of the season. But Cubs skipper Leo Durocher still wasn't convinced.

The patient, even-keeled, and restrained Hodges stood in stark contrast to Durocher's impatience, ill temperament, and assertiveness. Durocher famously said, "Nice guys finish last." Hodges would make good on debunking it.

The three-game set with Chicago at Shea Stadium in early July featured a thrilling ninth-inning comeback victory along with Seaver's brush with perfection. Chicago easily took the finale, prompting a typically glib response from Durocher after being asked by a reporter if the public had just seen the real Cubs: "No, those were the real Mets."

This stayed true for the remainder of the month. Real leadership exposes itself in bad times—not in good. Hodges's command shone through as the Mets appeared ready to fade from the race.

On July 30, he trudged slowly out to left field and inquired about the health of Cleon Jones, who had pursued a base hit too slowly for Hodges's preference. Hodges publicly pulled Jones, a .346 hitter and recent All-Star starter. Even though it's been claimed that this was nothing more than a manager removing his ailing player, the perception permeated throughout the team. Nobody was exempt from protocol. Jones later called it a galvanizing moment. But the Mets weren't stirred right away.

Instead, it was a clubhouse lecture on August 13, following the seventh loss in 11 games, that lit a fire. Players responded to this edict by embarking on a rousing 37-11 finish to the regular season. Hodges's calculated intensity sparked a resurgence.

The Mets were less prone to wilt in the summer heat thanks to age and Gil's insistence on tinkering the lineup, while Durocher's proclivity to put out the same starting lineup of veteran Cubs in the constant daytime heat of light-less Wrigley Field began to show. So when the Mets gained a second wind in August and took 21 of 31, the Cubs entered September with their tongues dragging and gasping for air.

The Mets were in no mood to lend any oxygen. New York swept Chicago in a two-game set and, soon after, snatched command of the NL East. On their way to the division title, New York went 23-7 over the final month in complete contrast to the Cubs' 8-18 plunge. *These* were the real Mets.

Advancing to the inaugural best-of-five League Championship Series, the West champion Braves possessed four future Hall of Famers and a right-handed-heavy pitching staff. Hodges saw no reason to change his platoon strategy. The lefty quartet of Art Shamsky, Wayne Garrett, Ken Boswell, and Ed Kranepool helped New York compile 27 runs in a three-game sweep.

But as easily as the Mets pushed aside the Braves, there was little belief they could take down an Orioles team that had won 109 regular-season contests. After an opening-game defeat that momentarily brought them back to earth, the Mets' starting arms showed why great pitching stops great hitting.

Clendenon, meanwhile, feasted on a lefty-heavy Baltimore rotation as the Mets answered the O's with three straight victories, quickly making converts in the process. Game 5 looked to be going Baltimore's way until Gil intervened.

The first pitch from Dave McNally in the bottom of the sixth dove in on Cleon Jones and rolled toward the Mets dugout. Jones began walking to first base, sure it hit him in the foot, before home plate umpire Lou DiMuro called him back. Hodges stoically approached DiMuro and presented what turned out to be indisputable evidence—a ball with a small smudge of shoe polish. Just like his players did, DiMuro took Hodges at his word. Jones went to first base.

The soon-to-be-named series MVP Clendenon then belted his third home run to pull New York to within a run. Al Weis, everything but a power threat, followed in the seventh with the game-tying homer. It was then that manager Earl Weaver and his Orioles realized they were fighting a force greater than the Mets. A two-run eighth buried the Birds for good.

A year many feel was guided by the hands of baseball gods had reached its immaculate end.

The incredibility of that world championship led to the impossible task of delivering an encore. Nothing, not even a repeat title, could live up to the events of the previous year. The 1970 Mets flirted with first place in mid-September then dropped 10 of their last 15 to end up six games short of Pittsburgh and in third place. New York's final record that season of 83-79 would be duplicated in 1971, except there was no pennant race to speak of.

The buttons Hodges pushed to sublime effect in 1969 didn't generate the same positive results, and attempts to improve an inadequate offense couldn't find traction.

Joe Foy, a Bronx native acquired at Hodges's behest to occupy third base, batted .236, battled drug problems, and was released after one season. Jim Fregosi, a six-time All-Star with the Angels, hit just .233 in 146 games. What made this trade so unfortunate was one of the main pieces sent in exchange for him: Nolan Ryan, who had yet to harness his control to the Mets' liking and subsequently wasn't keen on playing in such a big city. It would turn out to be one of the most lopsided deals in major-league history. Ryan struck out at least 300 batters in five of the next six years, threw four no-hitters in a three-year span (eventually reaching a record seven), and remained a premier flamethrower for more than two decades.

Conversely, the trade for Rusty Staub from Montreal was grade-A. Staub averaged 92 RBIs per every 162 games in his first four seasons in New York and added respectability to a lineup that was desperately in search of a bat like his. It was a trade that won over the public. It was also a trade Gil would never see pan out.

The strain of managerial responsibilities began to affect Hodges's health, most notably in 1968 when he missed the end of the regular season because of a heart attack caused by smoking. It was a wake-up call for Gil, as it would have been for anyone. Yet he maintained the habit.

On Easter Sunday 1972, shortly before the start of the regular season, Hodges collapsed and died suddenly from a second heart attack. It was a stunning blow to a team that had now lost its leader and to a baseball community in which he was so respected.

The Mets were quick to honor Hodges by retiring his number 14 the next year. The Hall of Fame voters haven't been as swift. If election is based on playing ability, integrity, sportsmanship, character, and contribution, then Hodges belongs there. He has many prominent advocates.

Vin Scully, who called games Gil played in his prime, said that Hodges's not being in Cooperstown "absolutely breaks my heart."

If you need more convincing, beyond what he did as a player, look no further than a man who credits him with shaping his own Hall of Fame career. "I loved Gil so much," Tom Seaver said. "I would've gotten in any foxhole with him. The thing that turned this franchise around and brought it respectability was Gil Hodges. He brought what we as young athletes—professional athletes—were missing was the understanding of the definition of professionalism ... and I carried that lesson for 19 years in the big leagues. Every place I went, every mound that I walked onto. Part of that in my heart, in my soul, and in my mind was Gil Hodges."

9

COACHES

DAVEY JOHNSON

He was part of Mets history well before he was part of the Mets. The final out of the 1969 World Series, a result of Jerry Koosman's pitch and Cleon Jones's catch, came off his bat. Seventeen years later, he reached the high point of his second baseball career, leading New York to its next championship.

Johnson foreshadowed his managerial future long before he took the Mets' reins. While playing in Baltimore, he enrolled in college mathematics courses during the offseason and derived formulas to determine the ideal Orioles lineup. Johnson combined classroom knowledge with on-field education from his manager, Earl Weaver.

Mets GM Frank Cashen was well aware of Johnson's studious qualities. He was in the Orioles front office during Johnson's playing days. The two had shared experiences in Baltimore, but shared little else. Writer Jack Lang compared their disparate personalities: "Johnson is outgoing and outspoken. Whereas Cashen weighs every word carefully when he answers a question, Johnson shoots from the hip."

Three years after Davey successfully navigated up the Mets' minor-league managerial chain, Cashen was ready to appoint him to his big-league club. Johnson assumed authority of a team that had been seriously lacking in conviction. Luckily, Davey never lacked in confidence. He marched to his own drumbeat and never pandered to be adored. Proof of that came even before his first season, when he went against Cashen's wishes.

Johnson was insistent on promoting 19-year-old Dwight Gooden, whom he had seen blow away the competition in Triple-A in 1983, to become his ace at the start of the '84 season. Cashen had felt the team should be a bit more cautious when it came to Gooden's development. Davey prevailed, and there was no second-guessing when Dr. K produced a legendary rookie season.

Self-awareness aside, Davey's managing style was more methodical. He had a Weaver-like mentality of planning moves well in advance. Johnson was neither conformist nor reactionary. There was always a process to his decision-making. Those processes usually resulted from computerized analytics to determine strengths and weaknesses—which, in the mid-1980s, was considered a new wave of managerial thinking.

But it certainly worked. Behind Gooden and Keith Hernandez, the Mets finished second at 90-72 in Davey's first year. With Gary Carter in the fold in 1985, New York inched closer, ending up at 98 victories and just a few games behind St. Louis.

The Mets had all the makings to bust loose, and Johnson knew it. He told his team in spring training it would dominate the rest of the league. These bold comments weren't confined to the privacy of the clubhouse. He expressed them to the media, too. Davey had reason to puff his chest out and make such a proclamation—he had a remarkably balanced roster with top-flight pitching and hitting. The players themselves took on the assertiveness of their manager. The '86 Mets embodied the city

Davey Johnson remains tops in Mets managerial victories and is the second-longest tenured.
JERRY COLI/DREAMSTIME

they represented with a flare and showmanship that fit in perfectly in New York but alienated those elsewhere.

Johnson directed an orchestra that rarely hit a false note. The Mets strutted to a huge division lead with complements of curtain calls and high-fives in large supply. Such outward brazenness was not lost on opponents. If they couldn't beat 'em, they'd try to beat 'em up.

And the Mets were all too willing to oblige. "We enjoy a fight," Davey said. "If that's what it takes, we'll fight every time."

Johnson's best use of baseball ingenuity came after Ray Knight and Kevin Mitchell packed a bit too much of a punch against the Reds. Short a position player in the wake of a wild brawl, Davey chose to put either Jesse Orosco or Roger McDowell, his two top relievers, in right field with the other on the mound and switch them depending on the situation. The Mets won that July 22 contest in Cincinnati—mere window dressing on the winningest regular season in franchise history. They finished with 108—tied for the most by a National League club in the modern era. But 108 wins would mean nothing without eight in the postseason.

From April through September, the Mets loudly justified Johnson's spring training boasts. In October, they showed the character that separates great teams from good ones. Throughout the LCS and World Series, the Mets were often cornered but never conquered. On five occasions, New York overcame deficits, including the clincher in the series with Houston and the final two World Series victories against Boston.

The Mets had reason to revel in their exhausting, 16-inning pennant-winning triumph over the Astros. But a champagne- and beer-infused clubhouse celebration was a tea party compared to what transpired on the flight home. Sportswriter Bob Klapisch referred to it as *Animal House* at 30,000 feet." The damages came back to Davey in the form of a hefty bill. He presented the bill at a team meeting—then ripped it to shreds, cementing his reputation as a player's manager.

The Mets escaped the Astros only to inhabit another crucible against Boston. New York lost the first two, both at Shea. Davey's solution for the off day? Take the day off. No hitting, no pitching, no fielding. Just rest.

Johnson knew he'd get heat from the media, believing it was an added sign of his arrogance. But criticism of his decision dissipated once the Mets kicked around Red Sox Game 3 starter Oil Can Boyd and scored four first-inning runs. New York won that night and took Game 4 the next. But a Game 5 defeat put them on the brink of failure. Another loss would mean a lost year.

Managers come under intense scrutiny for in-game decisions. If not for the 10th-inning rally in Game 6, Davey's choice to have Howard Johnson swing away in the ninth with runners on first and second with nobody out in a tie game would've justifiably put him squarely in the crosshairs.

Thus, we lament Sox skipper John McNamara's choices— to remove Roger Clemens in the seventh and to keep hobbling Bill Buckner on the field in the tenth instead.

Johnson's club stared defeat in the face and prevailed. The Mets danced through an easy regular season and survived a drama-filled postseason.

But reaching the pinnacle isn't as hard as staying there. Johnson's teams finished second twice in the next three years. Without the wild card to rely on, the Mets had to play within the stricture of a limited playoff field; and by those parameters, they underperformed.

The targets the Mets placed on their own backs with their swagger from '86 grew larger, with vengeful teams looking to bring the New Yorkers down a peg. But, in truth, the Mets mostly did it to themselves. The self-inflicted wounds included drug problems, infighting, injury, and under-achievement. More often the whole was less than the sum of its parts.

The friction between Cashen and Johnson amplified as their talent-laden teams weren't capable of living up to their full potential. Even during a division title run in 1988, Cashen scoffed about giving Johnson a new contract. Nonetheless, the Mets appeared ready for a return to the World Series, going up against a Dodgers team they manhandled during the regular season—winning 10 of 11 contests. Johnson's undoing came in Game 4, when he stuck with Dwight Gooden in the ninth inning following a walk instead of using lefty-throwing Randy Myers to face lefty-swinging Mike Scioscia. Gooden threw one pitch too many, and Scioscia tied a game the Mets would lose. New York would also lose the series in seven.

After another disappointing second-place showing in 1989, Cashen tested Johnson's loyalty and sanity by asking him to fire two close assistants. Bench coach Bud Harrelson was perceived as the manager-in-waiting with Johnson the manager-in-peril. The writing on the wall was clear when the Mets started slowly in 1990. Players were abusing the rules set in place, and Davey didn't possess the iron fist necessary to lay down the law when they were out of line.

Those who were able to provide leadership reinforcement in the clubhouse—specifically Keith Hernandez and Gary Carter—had departed. Communication issues with the front office, which had plagued him throughout his tenure, became even more prevalent. By May 29, with the team 20-22 and in fourth place, Johnson—who had never finished worse than second place and never with fewer than 87 wins—was given his walking papers.

Johnson's Mets will always be lamented for not living up to their enormous potential. But those clubs proved that having the best talent can bring its own set of challenges. Considering the pressure that engulfed him, Johnson kept his teams intact on his way to the most wins by any Mets manager.

BOBBY VALENTINE

It's hard to find someone with more baseball knowledge, and he'd be the first to tell you so. There are myriad ways to describe Bobby V's tenure with the Mets and Valentine in general. Boring is not one of them. Bobby V had a mixture of intellect and ego that made him—and the Mets during that same time—supremely fascinating.

Valentine was both sharp as a tack and as blunt as a kick to the groin. He held no predilection when it came to who he confronted: players, upper management, fellow managers, and the media.

His temperament, and everything that came with it, was destructive when the Mets were verging on catastrophe—like when they faded from the playoff picture in 1998 and then nearly did the same in 1999—and trivial when the Mets were thriving—like when they made the '99 NLCS and the 2000 World Series.

His overall record made such candor tolerable. The former star athlete from Stamford, Connecticut, won 88 or more games in each of his first four full seasons and finished his seven-season tenure 69 games above .500.

Valentine became the first Mets skipper to engineer back-to-back postseason appearances, but his finest work of managing might have been in 1997. After taking over for the fired Dallas Green at the tail end of 1996, Bobby improved a team

Equal parts brilliant and arrogant, Bobby Valentine managed 1,003 games, won 536 times, and was never boring.
JERRY COLI/DREAMSTIME

lacking a legitimate superstar by 17 wins and had them in wild card contention up until the final week.

The superstar void was filled by the May 1998 acquisition of Mike Piazza. But with such an acquisition comes raised expectations, and with expectations come the consequences of falling short. This tough reality arrived when the Mets dropped their final five games to end up one away from the National League Wild Card and finished with as many wins as they had in '97. The moves that had worked so brilliantly for Valentine for most of the year backfired when it mattered most.

While the playoff hopes for '98 were slammed shut at the very end, the 1999 Mets came to the point of death so often that it would've made Rasputin proud. The team was like Bobby himself: unpredictable and entertaining.

Never was this truer than on June 9. Valentine, who had been tossed from an extra-inning affair, returned to the Shea dugout wearing a T-shirt and disguised with glasses and a moustache.

"It's going to cost me a lot of money," he said to the press in the clubhouse afterwards. "I don't regret the fact that it lightened the team."

But the league wasn't amused. Valentine was fined $5,000 and suspended for two games.

It was an attempt to ease what had been a tense period and the height of the dysfunctional power dispute between Valentine and his younger general manager Steve Phillips.

Following an eight-game losing streak, Phillips dismissed his pitching coach, hitting coach, and bullpen coach in a passive-aggressive ploy to get Bobby to resign. Instead, with Valentine holding his ground, the Mets went 15-3 following the staff purge and thrust themselves back into playoff contention.

Bobby kept his job then but almost saw the ax in April 2000. Phillips strongly considered cutting Valentine after he found out about a strongly worded speech to University of

Pennsylvania students that was littered with direct shots at management.

Bobby had a way with words, even if he got carried away with them. And as the 1999 season was coming to a head, Valentine stirred the pot just when it was about to boil over.

The momentum from June carried through the summer, maintaining a pace that put the Mets at 34 games above .500 in mid-September. Then came a seven-game losing streak—six of them against Atlanta—that put their postseason chances on life support. Valentine's status as manager, which had never been fully secure, was seriously questioned. The media began to pick at the shortcomings of a skipper who had gone 1,700 games without reaching the postseason. His bevy of in-game maneuvers, bullpen machinations, and lineup changes, which were nothing more than Bobby's experimental nature, were now viewed as desperate ploys to stave off a second straight collapse.

Valentine offered himself up in an ultimatum, saying the organization should fire him if the Mets didn't recover. It was totally unconventional for a manager to independently place his head in the guillotine. But everyone should've known by then that Valentine never took the conventional route. It reflected the dogged optimism that would soon be exhibited by his players. The attempts to write the epitaph of the 1999 Mets were greeted with tremendous resistance.

Valentine's club needed to win two of three ending the regular season just to have a chance at the playoffs. It won all three, which set up a one-game playoff in Cincinnati. The Mets won that, too.

Then they had to take on Randy Johnson in Game 1 of the NLDS. They tagged the Hall of Famer for seven runs in a victory. Up 2-1 in the series, they persevered through an extra-inning affair in Game 4 to avoid having to face Johnson again back in Arizona. They won and were rewarded, if you will, with an NLCS date against the Braves.

Although close, the Mets dropped the first three. They seemed ripe to be swept. Not so. They scratched out a Game 4 win, then survived a six-hour, 15-inning, rain-soaked epic to take Game 5, capped by the "Grand Slam Single" from Robin Ventura.

"I've been in long games," said a mentally drained Valentine, who utilized a then-playoff-record nine pitchers to achieve a trip back to Atlanta. "But not games where every pitch meant so much."

With limited fresh arms in his arsenal, Valentine rolled the dice with his best big-game pitcher, Al Leiter, on short rest. What occurred was the worst possible outcome: six batters, no outs, and the Mets down five runs before coming to bat. New York incredibly rallied once more, but the weariness of the Mets pitchers finally caught up with them. Their bullpen couldn't hold one-run leads in the eighth and 10th. And finally, in the 11th, when Kenny Rogers walked Andruw Jones with the bases loaded, the resistance encountered its last stand.

"I told my guys after the game that it might be a shorter winter or a longer winter for them, but I thought they played like champions," Valentine said. "They should feel like champions."

Bobby had dispelled notions about his inability to lead in critical situations.

There were fewer doubts in 2000, when the franchise made its first repeat trip to the postseason and Valentine made his first venture to the World Series. Their ride to the playoffs dealt with far fewer hairpin curves than the year before. The Mets rather easily claimed the wild card (missing out on the division title by a game) with a mixture of accomplished veterans like Piazza, Ventura, Al Leiter, and John Franco along with unheralded journeymen like Rick Reed, Benny Agbayani, and Timo Pérez.

New York had slight trouble beating the Giants in the NLDS and even less difficulty dispensing with the Cardinals in the NLCS. There was little, if anything, about the Mets' five-game World Series loss to the Yankees that could be laid at Valentine's feet. Certainly not Pérez's misjudging of Todd Zeile's near home run in Game 1, which cost him an opportunity to score in what ended up a one-run defeat. Certainly not his closer, Armando Benítez, blowing a ninth-inning lead in the opener. And certainly not his top pitcher, Leiter, succumbing to Yankee resilience late in Game 5 after gutting out eight solid innings.

Valentine had his best season in 2000 but showed the best side of his character in September 2001. The terrorist attacks that devastated the city sounded a call to action that Bobby emphatically answered by tirelessly volunteering his time to be part of the relief effort.

The pennant race the Mets had entered because of a late-season surge was set on the backburner in favor of bringing the country back to normalcy. The meeting between the Mets and Braves on September 21, the first game in New York after 9/11, and a contest in which New York prevailed with Mike Piazza's eighth-inning homer, had a vastly different feel.

"That wasn't a game," Valentine said. "That was an event. That was the greatest event I ever had the opportunity to go to and be a part of."

It's rare for a manager to leave on his terms—or good terms. Valentine was no different.

His only losing year, marred by a lengthy home losing streak and rumors of clubhouse marijuana use, turned out to be his last. The Mets fired Valentine after 2002, from which he jetted off to future successes in Japan—leaving behind many triumphs, a few more enemies, and a legion of appreciative and entertained fans.

10

FRONT OFFICE

GENERAL MANAGER—FRANK CASHEN

On October 27, 1986, the rebuilding effort that began some six years prior came to fruition. Five of the nine Mets starters in Game 7 of the World Series were obtained through trades he orchestrated. Two others were drafted under his watch. And five of the remaining 16 on the roster were acquired by him either though player swaps or free agency. He also handpicked the manager. Needless to say, Frank Cashen's fingerprints were all over this championship blueprint.

His path to the Mets was unconventional and roundabout. The Baltimore native worked as a sportswriter, attorney, and public relations man at the raceway and brewery of Jerry Hoffberger until Hoffberger bought the Orioles and asked Cashen to work for his baseball team in 1965. It turned out to be wonderful timing. Cashen oversaw two championships as executive vice president and then took the GM reins for five seasons beginning in 1971.

Cashen left the O's to return to Hoffberger's brewery, then moved on to become an administrator of Major League Baseball and seemed content to stay there until early 1980. That's when new Mets owner Nelson Doubleday talked Cashen back into the front office.

He would be granted total control of the organization—serving as both general manager and chief operating officer. But the organization he inherited was in tatters, coming off three straight last-place finishes before abominably low attendance figures and a farm system bereft of much promising talent. This was not your typical rebuilding project. As Cashen later called it, this was a "total upheaval."

It was a chore altogether daunting and delectable to a personnel guru seeking a challenge. The Mets were an ideal project to put his acumen to the test. Cashen promised a turnaround but not within an exact timetable.

"I can't tell you how long it's going to take to win a pennant," he said at his introductory press conference. "I think we're going to win a pennant. If I didn't really feel that way, I wouldn't have taken the job in the first place."

The task at hand would be peppered with second-guessing from the New York media and cries from impatient fans. But there would be no such qualms with Cashen's first important decision. By virtue of the league lead in losses in 1979, the Mets were granted the luxury of selecting first in the following year's amateur draft. Even more fortunate, the top pick was supremely easy: Darryl Strawberry, the high school phenom from Los Angeles and a "can't miss" prospect who was the building block upon which Cashen could construct his future.

Strawberry needed years to ripen, so Cashen continued to revamp the minor-league system by stockpiling prospects and bringing up those ready for the majors—like exciting youngsters Mookie Wilson and Hubie Brooks. Cashen also tried to build through trades, which didn't work too well at first. Ellis Valentine and George Foster both proved to be past their prime. Local product Lee Mazzilli was shipped out to

Frank Cashen resurrected the Mets starting in the early 1980s and built the 1986 championship roster.
NATIONAL BASEBALL HALL OF FAME

fan disapproval in 1982. But in that exchange came Ron Darling, still blossoming in the minor leagues, and this began a sequence of shrewd deals that would transform the Mets into bona fide contenders.

One year later, Cashen executed his finest move: fleecing the Cardinals into giving up clutch-hitting, elite-fielding Keith Hernandez for Neil Allen and Rick Ownbey at the trade deadline. Then, in the winter of 1984, he pried away Gary Carter from his beloved Montreal for Brooks, Mike Fitzgerald, Floyd Youmans, and Herm Winningham.

The acquisition of veteran leaders along with the progression of Strawberry would be joined by pitching prodigy Dwight Gooden. By the middle of the decade, the wealth of talent assembled by the Mets had them primed for long-term success. But this plan wouldn't reach its goal if it didn't have the right man keeping it together. Fortunately, the type of person he wanted was already in his organization.

Cashen said of Davey Johnson, whom he promoted from Triple-A Tidewater to become Mets skipper in '84: "We needed a younger manager. A manager that, perhaps, communicated a little better with the younger ballplayers. A manager that was not afraid to take a chance."

The GM and his field general occasionally battled each other, but more importantly, the Mets were battling the elites of the National League. New York positioned itself into the Eastern Division race in each of Johnson's first two seasons, but ultimately were runners-up both times.

New York had very little that needed fixing after a 98-win season in 1985. But leaving nothing to chance, Cashen set out to fulfill two goals that winter: get a right-handed-hitting second baseman to complement Wally Backman and acquire a pitcher for the back end of the rotation. Former Minnesota Twin Tim Teufel filled the second base need and allowed Backman to bat .340 from the left side in '86.

Bob Ojeda, acquired from Boston, added to the embarrassment of pitching riches. He outdid projections, leading the team in wins (18), placing second in the National League in ERA (2.57), and tossing seven complete games as his off-speed stuff melded splendidly with the fastball-heavy staff of Gooden, Darling, and Sid Fernandez.

Cashen had built a monstrous roster that lived up to its potential in 1986 by winning the World Series in a fashion more dramatic than anyone anticipated. But he might've felt like Dr. Frankenstein. For while this Mets team resoundingly fulfilled his vision of six years earlier, its brashness—loved by locals and loathed by outsiders—went against Cashen's idea of winning with class. Nevertheless, he could take much of the credit for the on-field achievements.

"The reason the Mets are a success is Frank Cashen—no ifs, ands, or buts," Doubleday said following the World Series triumph.

And there was little reason to believe this wouldn't continue. A roster chock-full of veteran leaders and still-ascending stars, it had "dynasty" written all over it. But even before the team he built could pursue more rings, he unknowingly began chipping away at its foundation and character.

Ray Knight, the World Series MVP and feisty third baseman, was barely offered a chance to return. More damaging was the trade of Kevin Mitchell to San Diego in exchange for Kevin McReynolds. Mitchell was a budding star who the Mets wrongly believed was a bad influence on Dwight Gooden and Darryl Strawberry. And while McReynolds was by no means a wasted commodity, the losses of Mitchell and Knight created a void of the mental toughness and attitude that the '86 Mets were so noted for.

Cashen further stripped the identity when he jettisoned Backman to Minnesota, then Lenny Dykstra and Roger McDowell to Philadelphia. He had undervalued firebrands and overvalued minor-league standouts like Gregg Jefferies, who was incapable of handling the pressures of New York.

While Cashen's Mets remained competitive, they would never return to the World Series, each time falling short of expectations. Following the World Series victory, the Mets had two second-place finishes and a disappointing loss to the Dodgers in the '88 NLCS. The flame that burned so brightly in '86 had begun to diminish. In May 1990, Cashen dismissed Davey Johnson in favor of Bud Harrelson, citing a team-wide lack of focus.

"We have been underachievers for some period of time now," he said on the day of the firing. The Mets would gather themselves to finish second again, only to unravel as the 1991 season reached its second half. By now, it was apparent the dynasty that should have been would never be. Cashen relinquished the day-to-day operations at year's end to Al Harazin, who was helpless in trying to mend a dysfunctional franchise without a magic wand or much baseball acumen. Under Harazin, the Mets completely came apart, losing 90 games in 1992 before bottoming out at 103 defeats in 1993.

For the great amount of credit that must be bestowed upon Cashen for taking a dilapidated franchise and constructing it into a winner, he also must accept liability for allowing future decisions to slowly dismantle the championship framework he constructed. But what he built, resulting in a collection of talent far superior to any other period in Mets history, deserves to be justly recognized.

OWNER—JOAN PAYSON

She was visible without being meddlesome; fervent about her team, but kindhearted about her players; and lived in royal splendor while still exuding a common touch.

Proving baseball is a pastime that conjoins varied lifestyles and backgrounds, Payson's love of the sport and devotion to the Mets were mirrored by those who paid for tickets to root for them.

Ownership of New York's National League franchise was one of many opulent indulgences she enjoyed. In addition to her selfless contributions to many charitable causes, she owned a horse stable, was a trustee of the Metropolitan Museum of Art and the Museum of Modern Art, and a contributor to both New York Hospital and North Shore University Hospital. Despite her wealth and high social status, Payson was "unspoiled and unaffected" to those closely associated with her.

As a branch of the wealthy Whitney family tree, Joan inherited $100 million from her father in the late 1920s and set out to make the most of her riches.

Payson's deep expendable income allowed her to purchase roughly 10 percent of the New York Giants—the team she grew up following. But by 1957, looking to boost attendance and revenue, the Giants had entertained the possibility of moving west. Only Payson and fellow stockholder M. Donald Grant—also her stockbroker and investment advisor—opposed the change. Despite their wishes, Major League Baseball approved the relocation of the Giants to San Francisco, concurrent with the Dodgers transferring to Los Angeles.

The demands for a replacement team in New York, forged by Bill Shea, convinced MLB to expand. With Payson selected as principal owner of the new National League club, she became the first woman to purchase a major sports franchise. As expected, she had a hand in many early administrative tasks. Payson chose "Metropolitans" as the team name, Grant as chairman, and former Yankees general manager George Weiss as team president.

Weiss and Payson understood that the ideal way to cater to National League supporters and New York baseball fans, deprived of the Dodgers and Giants, was to plug the roster with notable, albeit aging, stars like Duke Snider, Don Zimmer, Richie Ashburn, and Gil Hodges. The same principle held true when they tapped 72-year-old Casey Stengel as manager.

The lovable matriarch of the Mets, Joan Payson purchased the expansion franchise upon its birth.
NATIONAL BASEBALL HALL OF FAME

While this mixture of graybeards and unproven recruits was a formula for on-field futility, it instituted a loyalty that has spanned generations of Mets fans. Support never wavered despite an average of 105 losses over their first seven seasons and neither did Payson's dedication to cultivate a warm, endearing atmosphere for her players.

"She radiated friendship," said Ed Kranepool. "She made you feel like you were around your grandmother. That's the type of person she was."

According to author Matt Silverman, Payson's stewardship during a transitional time, as owning a team became less a source of income and more a side business or hobby.

"She wasn't really a hands-on owner," Silverman said. "But at that point, a lot of men who owned teams weren't either. She was the team's lovable matron and was content to go to meetings and make sales pitches."

Payson found greater comfort being among the crowd in a box seat rather than isolating herself in the relative solitude of a suite. Payson's lifestyle was too lavish for most to imagine, but she fit right in with the loyalists who filled the Polo Grounds and later Shea Stadium.

She also was no less superstitious than ordinary fans. When the Mets embarked on their run to the 1969 NL East title, it came as a positively stunning development to those who were witness to seven years of cellar-dwelling. Count Payson among the amazed. She had made plans to travel to Europe that September. But out of fear of jinxing her team, she refused to alter her itinerary. Payson returned from Europe in time to witness the World Series victory firsthand and accept the Commissioner's Trophy in the locker room.

Upon her death at age 72 in October 1975, Payson's funeral attendance reflected her array of interests and selfless generosity. "There's no words to describe that lady," said Willie Mays, considered to be Payson's favorite player and who was given a chance to return to New York in the twilight of his career. "She was just a wonderful person."

The controls of the franchise were passed on to her daughter, Lorinda de Roulet, who had far less interest in baseball operations. De Roulet divested herself of the club in 1980, but her mother's legacy wouldn't be forgotten. That same year, Payson became an inaugural inductee into the Mets Hall of Fame.

11

HONORABLE MENTIONS

Pitchers

Sid Fernandez

"El Sid"—an optical illusion. A deceptive downward motion that often ended in a rising fastball. You'd swear he was throwing uphill. With 6.85 hits per nine innings, only three others who registered more than 1,500 frames allowed fewer: Nolan Ryan, Sandy Koufax, and Clayton Kershaw. His batting average against was regularly among the lowest from 1985 through 1993—the years he spent in New York. During that same span, he averaged 8.5 strikeouts every nine innings. This normally would make Sid an ace on the Mets or any other team, but his weight and stamina contributed to occasional control issues as games progressed. Endurance was not a requirement in his most important appearance as a Met—when he delivered 2.1 hitless innings of relief in the finale of the 1986 World Series and prevented the Red Sox from adding to their 3–0 lead. Fernandez energized the Shea crowd and rejuvenated a Mets offense that would later awaken and overtake Boston for the title. Ray Knight was series MVP, but Sid was the key to a Game 7 win.

David Cone

General baseball fans know him for his perfect game in Yankee pinstripes in 1999 and for contributing to five World Series victories, four with that team from the Bronx. But in 17 big-league seasons, Cone won more games, had a better ERA, and threw more strikeouts as a Met. His finest year, 1988, began with Cone excluded from a stocked Mets rotation. Rick Aguilera's injury in early May became Cone's opportunity. He shot to the top of New York's staff with a 20-3 record, leaving the National League wondering how another power arm found its way to Flushing. Even more perplexed were the Royals, the team that dealt Cone to New York in 1986. Twice Cone led the NL in strikeouts, including a tally of 241 in 1991. The last 19 came on the final day of the season in Philadelphia, matching Tom Seaver's single-game record. Cone was freed from a raging dumpster fire in 1992 when he was sent to Toronto, where he found serenity and, soon after, the first of his handful of championship rings.

Roger McDowell

He brought new meaning to the term "comic relief." McDowell fooled 'em on the mound with his deceptive sinkerball and had 'em laughing in the dugout with his zany antics. The leading practitioner of the hot foot, among other pranks, designated him as the recurrent class clown. When his part-time funnyman gig gave way to his full-time reliever role, he didn't mess around. His five shutout innings in Game 6 of the 1986 NLCS preserved a 3–3 tie through the 13th. His success from the pennant-winning series against Houston diminished with a subpar World Series, although he's credited with the Game

7 victory. McDowell's high-leverage playoff situations were preceded with a heavy dose of regular-season assignments—entering 75 times, being involved in 23 decisions, and winning 14. Splitting save opportunities with lefties Jesse Orosco and Randy Myers, McDowell locked down 84 games from 1985 to 1989.

Armando Benítez

Closers are to baseball as kickers are to football. Their performance—and, ultimately, their fate—gets measured through fleeting pressure-filled moments. Benítez was not immune to high-leverage failures that drove fans to intense fury. Where to begin? Try Game 1 of the 2000 World Series and the two spectacular September 2001 meltdowns against the Braves. Sorry if any of those provoke a migraine. Then there are the lesser—yet still biting—pains that contribute to some sort of PTSD—which made every ensuing flirtation with disaster a call for fans to renew their indigestion medication prescription. Those aggravations almost negate his 160 saves in nearly five seasons. Twice he established a then-franchise record for single-season saves (41 in 2000 and 43 in 2001). But when you're a shutdown pitcher in the same town as Mariano Rivera, there's instant inferiority. The 89 percent save rate Benítez established from 1999 through 2002 is the identical ratio at which Rivera closed games during that same span. But it's the important regular-season games and the postseason scenarios where judgment is made and where a line of demarcation is drawn. It's not how many you save, it's when you save them.

Catchers

John Stearns

He might have been better suited to being a linebacker than a backstop. Before protecting the plate was a task that required the sturdiness of a brick wall instead of the nimbleness of a bullfighter, Stearns didn't back away from contact. In fact, he embraced it. "Bad Dude," as he was known, made four All-Star appearances between 1978 and 1982. But in an era in which the Mets were lucky to be sending one or two representatives to the Midsummer Classic, these were by no means token gestures. Following in the mold of Jerry Grote, Stearns ruggedly withstood the occupational hazards of catching over 11 seasons (10 with New York) before his body broke down. Stearns was exceptionally quick for a catcher, setting a major-league record for the position with 25 stolen bases in 1977. His best offensive season came the next year, during which he hit 15 homers and tallied 73 RBIs.

Todd Hundley

Recognition for Hundley was established with a two-year power stretch as impressive as any Met has ever produced. His 41 home runs in 1996, likely aided by the performance-enhancing drug use made known in the 2008 release of the Mitchell Report, eclipsed the single-season high for catchers (previously held by Brooklyn Dodger legend Roy Campanella) while also setting a Mets club record. Both marks have since been topped, but he followed that year with 30 homers for 1997, on his way to amassing the most round-trippers by a Met during the 1990s. A career-threatening elbow injury, a war of words with manager Bobby Valentine, and the acquisition of Mike Piazza in 1998 marked the beginning of the end of his time in New York. An experiment to insert him in left field later that year turned into an abject failure.

FIRST BASEMEN

Carlos Delgado

Several times, the Mets have been the benefactors of the Marlins' high-priced offloading: Al Leiter and Mike Piazza in 1998 and then Delgado in November 2005. Florida agreed to take on Mike Jacobs, Yusmeiro Petit, and Grant Psomas and loaned New York a new cleanup hitter. Delgado responded with 38 homers and 114 RBIs as the Mets ran away with the 2006 NL East crown. For a three-year stretch (2006–08), he, Carlos Beltrán, David Wright, and José Reyes combined to create the most potent lineup in the National League and perhaps the best offense in franchise history. Hip ailments eventually brought Delgado's career to a halt in early 2009 with 104 home runs and 339 RBIs over 468 games. Less than a year earlier, on June 27, 2008, he enjoyed his finest day as a major leaguer. In a 15–6 dismantling of the Yankees, Delgado hit a two-run double, a grand slam, and a three-run shot to establish a Mets single-game record of nine RBIs.

Ed Kranepool

On September 22, 1962, just 40 professional games and 17 life years under his belt, the Bronx native made his MLB debut around he received his high school diploma. On September 30, 1979, 1,853 major-league games and 18 seasons later, he doubled in his final at-bat. Kranepool's 1,418 hits remained the standard in Mets history for over three decades. Linking the

of 185 hits during the pennant-winning season. He'd break his own mark in 1975 with 191 while also setting a team-high with 37 doubles. If not for a vicious body slam from Pittsburgh's Ed Ott during a fight in 1977, which effectively ended his career, it's likely Millán's credentials would've been enhanced enough to earn a spot on this all-time team.

Third Baseman

Wayne Garrett

Even if the Mets didn't know it, Garrett turned out to be the closest thing to hot corner continuity from the late 1960s through the mid-1970s. Garrett's 709 games at the position made him the standard bearer for third-base occupancy over the better part of the next two decades. However, even though the red-haired 21-year-old's versatility in 1969 impressed the manager and the press, the Mets still looked elsewhere for players who would garner a majority of the playing time: first shipping off Amos Otis for troubled Joe Foy and later sending Nolan Ryan west for the frequently fragile Jim Fregosi. They were better off having more faith in Garrett's abilities. He had enough speed on the 1973 team to fill the leadoff spot and enough power to hit a career-high 16 homers (along with two more in the World Series). Garrett would patrol third base for more than 80 percent of the games that season and again the next.

Shortstop

Rey Ordoñez

Ordoñez entered the league in 1996 having already drawn comparisons to the greatest defensive shortstop ever, Ozzie Smith. It only took until the seventh inning of Opening Day, against Smith's St. Louis Cardinals no less, for Rey to show off his fielding wizardry—a relay throw from the outfield grass on his knees to prevent a key run from scoring. Ordoñez could be counted on to make the spectacular plays as well as the routine ones. He won three consecutive Gold Glove Awards beginning in 1997. And in 1999, he committed only four errors and led all National League shortstops in defensive WAR. Starting on June 13, 1999, and ending on March 30, 2000, Rey was flawless—establishing a major-league-record 101-game errorless streak. As spectacular as Ordoñez was at stopping runs, he found great difficulty producing them. His on-base percentage over his seven years as a Met was a paltry .290, he batted just .245, only stole 28 bases on 50 attempts, and his OPS was nearly 200 points lower than the average big leaguer at the time.

OUTFIELDERS

Kevin McReynolds

He never was a fan favorite and never commanded attention as many of his dynamic teammates did, despite being a reliable and consistent performer in his best years. And if you know McReynolds, he probably preferred it that way. The laconic Arkansas native was not prone to verbosity. His perceived attitude had the look of someone who played baseball as if it was an obligation, which made it easy to paint McReynolds as disinterested. Therefore, appreciation of a 26–home run and 90-RBI average over his first four seasons, dependable defense in left field, and deceptively effective baserunning didn't come easily. McReynolds immediately became one of the anchors of the Mets lineup in 1987 with a year that included career bests in homers (29), doubles (32), and hits (163). He followed that in

1988 with a .288 average, 27 home runs, and 99 runs driven in, finishing second on the team to Darryl Strawberry in all three categories. But he was far superior defensively, as his NL-leading 18 assists will attest. McReynolds also tallied 21 stolen bases without getting caught.

Yoenis Céspedes

Céspedes has been a walking game of "Operation." It's not if he'll get hurt but when. This exercise in consternation is the price paid for what a healthy Céspedes could deliver. It crystallized after he was acquired by the Mets at the 2015 trade deadline—an event that didn't go by without some anxious moments. Nabbed from the Tigers, the Mets didn't regret it. Céspedes performed like he was capable of doing, transforming a once-powerless lineup into one that carried the Mets to the front of a pennant race. Fifty-seven games, 17 home runs, and 44 RBIs later, New York was NL East champions. Coming off a World Series appearance, the Mets pinned their future on the flashy outfielder with seemingly many good years ahead. But since re-signing and extending his contract, his body hasn't allowed him to perform to a tremendous extent. From 2016 to 2018, Céspedes made a little more than 1,000 at-bats over 251 games with 57 homers and 157 runs driven in.

Dave Kingman

Many hitters swing for the fences. Kingman swung for the moon. "Kong" arrived with a bang—36 of them, actually, in 1975. That was a Mets single-season home run record which stood for just 12 months, because he broke it the next year with 37 (despite a thumb injury that held him to 123 games). His towering drives were as majestic and marvelous to watch as his abundance of strikeouts. Kingman whiffed 288 times over those same two seasons. Traded on the same night as the infamous Tom Seaver deal, Kingman returned in 1981—supplying more moonshots and more cool breezes while maintaining a boorish, moody behavior and defensive ineptness. He hit 22 homers and fanned a National League-high 105 times during a strike-shortened 100-game season. In '82, he held the league lead in both round-trippers (37) and strikeouts (156), and he batted .204—a lower average than Cy Young winner Steve Carlton. It took only 664 games for Kingman to reach 154 home runs, which remains fifth on the team's all-time list.

Lenny Dykstra

You wouldn't want him as your financial advisor, but you'd love him on your baseball team. Lit dynamite in human form, Dykstra retained a fiery intensity that stoked the Mets for five seasons. Lenny showed he was impervious to pressure and even liable to muscle up come October. For a player who averaged seven home runs during his big-league career Dykstra hit three postseason homers in the '86 playoffs, each of which was vital to the Mets' fortunes: a walk-off in Game 3 of the NLCS against Houston, a leadoff homer in Game 3 of the World Series at Fenway Park (after the Mets had dropped the first two at home), and another in the seventh inning of Game 4 that helped New York even the series. Bothered by being platooned with Mookie Wilson in center field, Dykstra pestered Mets management to make him a full-time contributor. The foolish solution was to send both him and Roger McDowell to Philadelphia for Juan Samuel. It drew instant criticism—only to grow louder when Samuel bombed and Dykstra shone as an everyday player for the Phillies.

Lee Mazzilli

His career began in the right place—just not at the right time. The Brooklyn native dreamt of playing in front of his hometown fans. Unfortunately, Mets support was difficult to find when Maz initially occupied center field. With nothing to cling to in the aftermath of Tom Seaver's departure, it was Mazzilli who became the focal point on a team going nowhere. As one of the lone bright lights during the dark ages, glorified as a local savior and matinee idol, too much was expected of a player who truthfully wasn't capable of being a superstar—although he averaged 16 homers and 72 RBIs from 1978 to 1980 and made his lone All-Star appearance in 1979, the only year he hit better than .300. The Mets used him as a trading chip in their rebuilding effort. Maz languished in baseball purgatory while New York developed into a contender. That was until 1986, when time and place blended perfectly. The Mets signed Mazzilli in August in a far different capacity. As a role player, he delivered key pinch-hits in the final games of the World Series.

ACKNOWLEDGMENTS

No book project is done in solitude—it just feels that way sometimes. I was extremely fortunate to have so many provide the support that made this possible. The first and most significant debt of gratitude is owed to Niels Aaboe, the senior acquisitions editor who approached me with the opportunity to take on this assignment. I'm extremely thankful he did, and I appreciate his patience while trudging through the first draft of the manuscript.

An additional thanks goes to production editor Meredith Dias, who guided me through the final stages and was always ready to answer my questions. The proofreading and copyediting processes are tedious and time-consuming. So to the editors at Lyons Press, thank you for helping convert my errors into hits. To my standby editors—aka friends, family members, and colleagues—you were an immense help and came through during a stressful time: Joseph Balkoski, Ed Beach, Rosemary Brown Wright, Matt Tick, Mark Rankin, and Inga Broksas.

My dad, Bill Wright, read over many chapters and used his photographic memory of events that happened well before I was alive to be a most essential fact-checker. A Mets fan since the Mets' birth, he took me to my first game in 1992 and probably had no idea the monster he was creating. To my mom, Susan Masterson, who went along with me to Shea Stadium and Citi Field and allowed me to pursue my love of baseball even if it wasn't in her best interest.

My tiny brain can only grasp so many recollections and statistics, so thank goodness for the existence of sites like Baseball-Reference, Retrosheet, and Ultimate Mets Database. I'm equally as appreciative to colleagues who conveyed their past book writing experiences and lent their tremendous insight over the years: Matthew Silverman, Greg Prince, Erik Sherman, Mark Healey, and Roland Lazenby.

Additional research for this book was done through interviews, which helped shape the narratives of the stories in this book: Jon Matlack, Frank Viola, Frank Thomas, Art Shamsky, Gil Hodges Jr., and Jerry Koosman. My great appreciation to the Baseball Hall of Fame and Museum, Sharon Chapman, and Buddy Weiss for providing photos that helped these words come to life.

I'd be remiss if I didn't make special mention of the 2019 Mets, who came to life when I was in the stressful stages of developing this manuscript and became a welcome distraction while further epitomizing the joy, hope, sorrow, and angst of following this team.

And lastly, to Natalie Beach—my part-time editor, part-time sounding board, and full-time supporter—who gave me more encouragement than I could ever dream of and was more patient than I could ever hope to be. If that wasn't enough, she temporarily put her longtime Orioles allegiance aside to become invested in the range of emotions that being a Mets fan entails. She can't say I didn't warn her.

SOURCES

BOOKS

Allen, Maury. *After the Miracle: The Amazin' Mets—Two Decades Later*. New York: St. Martin's Press, 1989.

Berkow, Ira. *Summers at Shea: Tom Seaver Loses His Overcoat and Other Mets Stories*. Chicago: Triumph Books, 2013.

Bjarkman, Peter. *The New York Mets Encyclopedia*. New York: Sports Publishing, 2013.

Blatt, Howard. *Amazin' Met Memories*. Tampa, FL: Albion Press, 2002.

Breslin, Jimmy. *Can't Anybody Here Play This Game?: The Improbable Saga of the New York Mets' First Year*. New York: Viking Press, 1963.

Coffey, Wayne. *They Said It Couldn't Be Done*. New York: Crown Archetype, 2019.

Cohen, Stanley. *A Magic Summer: The Amazin' Story of the 1969 New York Mets*. New York: Skyhorse Publishing, 2009.

Darling, Ron, with Daniel Paisner. *Game 7, 1986: Failure and Triumph in the Biggest Game of My Life*. New York: St. Martin's Press, 2016.

Ferry, David. *Total Mets: The Definitive Encyclopedia of the New York Mets' First Half-Century*. Chicago: Triumph Books, 2012.

Garry, Michael. *Game of My Life: Memorable Stories of Mets Baseball*. New York: Sports Publishing, 2015.

Harrelson, Bud, with Phil Pepe. *Turning Two: My Journey to the Top of the World and Back with the New York Mets*. New York: St. Martin's Press, 2012.

Honig, Donald. *The New York Mets: The First Quarter Century*. New York: Crown Publishers, 1986.

James, Bill. *The New Bill James Historical Baseball Abstract*. New York: Simon & Schuster, 2003.

Johnson, Davey, and Peter Golenbock. *Bats*. New York: Putnum, 1986.

Johnson, Davey, and Erik Sherman. *Davey Johnson: My Wild Ride in Baseball and Beyond*. Chicago: Triumph Books, 2018.

Kalinsky, George. *The New York Mets: A Photographic History*. New York: Macmillan, 1995.

Klapisch, Bob, and John Harper. *The Worst Team Money Could Buy: The Collapse of the New York Mets.* New York: Random House, 1993.

Lang, Jack, and Peter Simon. *The New York Mets: Twenty-Five Years of Baseball Magic.* New York: Henry Holt, 1986.

Markusen, Bruce. *Tales from the New York Mets Dugout: A Collection of the Greatest Mets Stories Ever Told.* New York: Sports Publishing, 2012.

McGraw, Tug, with Don Yeager. *Ya Gotta Believe!: My Roller-Coaster Life as a Screwball Pitcher, and Part-Time Father, and My Hope-Filled Fight Against Brain Cancer.* New York: New American Library, 2004.

Nowlin, Bill, and Brian Wright, eds. *Met-rospectives: A Collection of the Greatest Games in New York Mets History.* Phoenix, AZ: Society for American Baseball Research, 2018.

Pearlman, Jeff. *The Bad Guys Won!* New York: HarperCollins, 2004.

Prince, Greg W. *Faith and Fear in Flushing: An Intense Personal History of the New York Mets.* New York: Skyhorse Publishing, 2009.

Rose, Howie, and Phil Pepe. *Put It in the Book!* Chicago: Triumph Books, 2013.

Samelson, Ken, and Matthew Silverman, eds. *The Miracle Has Landed: The Amazin' Story of How the 1969 Mets Shocked the World.* Hanover, MA: Elm Street Press, 2009.

Shamsky, Art, and Erik Sherman. *After the Miracle: The Lasting Brotherhood of the '69 Mets.* New York: Simon & Schuster, 2019.

Sherman, Erik. *Kings of Queens: Life Beyond Baseball with the '86 Mets.* New York: Berkley, 2016.

Silverman, Matthew. *100 Things Mets Fans Should Know & Do Before They Die.* Chicago: Triumph Books, 2016.

———. *New York Mets: 50 Amazin' Seasons.* Minneapolis: MVP Books, 2011.

———. *Shea Stadium Remembered: The Mets, the Jets, and Beatlemania.* Guilford, CT: Lyons Press, 2019.

Sowell, Mike. *One Pitch Away: The Players' Stories of the 1986 LCS and World Series.* South Orange, NJ: Summer Game Books, 1995.

Wilson, Mookie, with Erik Sherman. *Mookie: Life, Baseball, and the '86 Mets.* New York: Berkley, 2014.

Zachter, Mort. *Gil Hodges: A Hall of Fame Life.* Lincoln: University of Nebraska Press, 2015.

FILMS

100 Winning Ways: 1988 Mets Highlights
1969 World Series Highlights
1973 World Series Highlights
1986 Mets: A Year to Remember
1986 World Series Highlights
1989 Mets Highlights
The 1990 New York Mets
Accent on Youth: 1977 Mets Yearbook
Amazin' Again: The Official 1999 New York Mets Highlight Video
An Amazin' Era
Fifteen Years of Fun: 1976 Mets Yearbook
The Greatest League Championship Series
Meet the Mets: 1975 Mets Yearbook
New York Mets: 50 Greatest Players
You Gotta Believe: 1973 Mets Yearbook

PERIODICALS

Associated Press
Baltimore Sun
Baseball Digest
Los Angeles Times
Newsday
New York Daily News
New York Post
New York Times
New York Mets Programs and Yearbooks, 1986–2018
The New Yorker
Sporting News
Sports Illustrated

RADIO

WCBS
WFAN

TELEVISION

ESPN
ESPN Classic
SNY
WCBS

WEBSITES

Amazinavenue.com
Baseballhall.org
Baseball-reference.com
Centerfieldmaz.com
ESPN.com
Faithandfearinflushing.com
Fangraphs.com
Medium.com
MetsmerizedOnline.com
Newyork.cbslocal.com
Ozy.com
SABR.org
SI.com
Ultimatemets.com
USAToday.com

YOUTUBE

"Mike & Mad Dog Reunion," youtube.com/
watch?v=CvEiLG66-r0&t=8632s.
"Mike Piazza Number Retirement Ceremony," youtube.com/
watch?v=_VkOOwzKoxc&t=816s.
"Playing for Peanuts: Episode 1," youtube.com/
watch?v=QdQdJ7K9M0Q&t=149s.
"Rusty Staub Visits Montreal," youtube.com/watch?v=vKgr_k3FULY.
"Shea Goodbye (Full Ceremony)," youtube.com/
watch?v=yBs6pRK1Wi0&t=1344s.
"1969 World Series, Game 5: Orioles at Mets," www.youtube.com/
watch?v=WbCWUehZKVU.
"1973 New York Mets: Road to the Pennant," youtube.com/
watch?v=_16efPkHvM0.
"1985 06 03 ABC MNB Mets at Dodgers," youtube.com/
watch?v=NznwkxuZDUU&t=8845s.
"1986 10 18 1986 World Series Game 1 Boston Red Sox at New York
Mets," youtube.com/watch?v=0LFyL_5JLcA&t=833s.
"1986 NLCS Game 6," youtube.com/watch?v=Ifbs2BioOBE.
"1986 World Series Game 7," youtube.com/watch?v=ZmODgrzd_b8.
"1988 10 12 1988 NLCS Game 7 New York Mets at Los Angeles Dodgers,"
youtube.com/watch?v=_bUtw7KCWkk&t=979s.
"1999 NLCS, Game 5: Braves at Mets," youtube.com/
watch?v=igrmzxcuCAQ.

ABOUT THE AUTHOR

Brian Wright is the author of *Mets in 10s: Best and Worst of an Amazin' History* and served as managing editor for *Metrospectives*, a publication from the Society for American Baseball Research (SABR) which chronicles the greatest games in franchise history. Brian has also contributed to other SABR books, including the most memorable moments in the history of the San Diego Padres, Wrigley Field, and old Comiskey Park. He currently resides in Washington, DC.